From Anathema to Dialogue

From Anathema to Dialogue

The Challenge of Marxist-Christian Cooperation

———◆———

ROGER GARAUDY

With replies by Karl Rahner, s.j.
and J. B. Metz

Collins
ST JAMES'S PLACE, LONDON
1967

This translation of *De l'Anatheme au Dialogue*
(first published in 1965 by Librairie Plon, Paris)
was made by Luke O'Neill

The translation of the German texts by Karl
Rahner, s.j. and J. B. Metz (first published in
1966 by Rowohlt Verlag G.M.B.H., Reinbek bei
Hamburg) was made by Edward Quinn

The translation of the text by Karl Rahner is
made by permission of Darton, Longman and
Todd Ltd.
The official version will appear in their forth-
coming publication *Theological Investigations*,
vol. 6

Printed in Great Britain by
Northumberland Press Limited
Gateshead

Preface

The Second Vatican Council, taking its lead from Pope John XXIII's encyclical *Pacem in terris*, has vigorously posed the question of the Church's dialogue with the world.

Now that the Council has come to an end, millions of men and women, both believers and unbelievers, look anxiously and hopefully towards Rome and wonder what the answer to this question will be. What canonical limitations will be placed on this dialogue, on the expectations it has aroused, on the prospects it has opened to us?

Pope John XXIII did not address his last encyclical solely to the clergy and faithful. Not limiting it to Catholics, he addressed it 'to all men of good will'. The decisions which are to be made affect each one of us, and on those decisions depend to some extent our countries' future and the world's.

It is, then, by no means presumptuous for a Marxist to answer in a fraternal manner the appeal fraternally addressed to all, and to ask a few questions of his own about the possibilities, the limitations and the perspectives of this dialogue, so as to offer his contribution to the common effort of reflection.

R.G.

Contents

Marxist Utopianism and Christian Hope

by Karl Rahner, s.j.

The theme assigned to me may be formulated as the Christian doctrine of man's future. It might be expressed more polemically as the difference between Christian eschatology and intra-mundane utopianism.

Two preliminary remarks may be permitted. Firstly, the human-Christian experience of God as such cannot also be expressly discussed here. This is a theme that must be presupposed. Of course, this presupposition can be so made as to indicate at the same time, at least implicitly, that the question of man's absolute future includes within itself the question of God: that a person, therefore, who makes himself open to his absolute future also experiences what is really meant by the word 'God'; and it is of secondary importance whether he uses this word or not, whether or not he explicitly reflects on this unity of absolute future and God.

Secondly, since even to give an account of Christian eschatology is really beyond the possibilities of a brief essay, what we called intra-mundane utopianism by contrast with Christian eschatology can be touched on only peripherally. What therefore remains untouched and left open to discussion is the question whether the Marxist expectation of the future is the direct opposite of the Christian doctrine of the absolute future of the individual human being and of mankind, whether then they directly contradict one another, *or* whether the Christian doctrine of the future really only fills an empty space left inevitably by the Marxist expectation of the future, since it aims merely at a possible, genuine, intra-mundane future of man—that is, one that can be categorically planned and foreseen—so that the Marxist denial of the Christian future, which naturally has to be a part of a dialectical materialism, is merely an external and separable complement to the draft of this intra-mundane future. Although here really only one thing has to be said—namely, that God exists as the absolute future for us—this one thing can be said only in several successive statements. From which it follows that each statement becomes completely intelligible only within the whole and that the reader must be asked to have patience.

1. *Christianity is a religion of the future*. It is understood and can be understood only from the standpoint of the future which it sees as an absolute, coming upon the individual man and upon mankind as a whole. Its interpretation of the past occurs in and through the progressive unveiling of the approaching future, and the sense and import of the present is explained in the light of a hope opened to the approach of the absolute future.

Christianity understands the world indeed from the standpoint of saving *history*: but this means that it is not really and in the last resort a doctrine of a static essence of the world and of man, always remaining the same and repeating itself in a space of time which as such is empty, without really advancing. It means the proclamation of an absolute becoming that does not go on into a vacuum, but really finds the absolute future, indeed already moves *within* it, because this becoming is *thus* really different from its outstanding future and fulfilment

12

(and therefore does not imply any pantheism); that nevertheless the infinite reality of this future holds sway in it, carries it on, as intrinsically effecting this becoming, while being itself independent of becoming. Thus any kind of primitive deism or theory of a purely external relation between God and world is surpassed from the very beginning and the truth *in* pantheism maintained.

The real essence of man can therefore be defined precisely as the possibility of attaining the absolute future: that is, not this or that particular state, which is always included again already in another and greater, still outstanding and yet existent future, thus being made relative and recognized as such. Christianity is therefore the religion of becoming, of history, of self-transcendence, of the future. For it, whatever exists, exists as a charge; everything is intelligible only in terms of what is still to be. The tendency towards the absolute future has indeed its reason, its standard, an essence behind it, which casts before it a horizon of the possible, a law which is followed. But since the final reason is the absolute fullness of the reality of God and the final goal precisely this God who appoints the beginning by making himself the goal, then any conception of essence and nature is indeed truly realistic solely if it is understood in the light of the future which alone reveals the beginning.

2. *Christianity is the religion of the absolute future.* What this means is really just what we have been saying. If man (and mankind) is the reality which in knowing and willing itself is always ahead of itself, which constitutes itself by drafting its future or—better—drafting its essence in relation to this very future (or—since it is a question of drafting the *absolute* future, which of its nature cannot really be planned and made—allowing this to come upon itself), then the decisive question for

a metaphysical anthropology is this: whether the future
towards which man projects himself is merely a categorial
one. That is to say such that its individual and diverse
elements restricted in space and time form this future in
a combination, eventually planned and manipulated,
eventually also more and more complex—*so* that this as
finite is in principle constantly included in a wider,
empty possibility of future *or* whether the unsurpassable
infinite future as such comes upon man, whether therefore the possible scope of the future and the future as
present become identical?

In regard to this question, Christianity opts for the
second possibility: the absolute future is the true and
proper future of man; *it* is for him real possibility, an
offer, that which comes upon him, which is in prospect,
its acceptance the ultimate function of his existence.
Since man can concern himself with a future that can be
produced, that has a space-time localization, that is made
up of parts of his world, only by encroaching on what
is fundamentally the whole of unlimited possibility,
there is always in his intra-mundane concern (at least
implicitly and often perhaps also repressed) the question
of the possible encounter with just this infinite whole as
such, with the absolute future. And this question Christianity answers in the sense that this absolute future is
not merely the ever-outstanding condition of the possibility of a categorial, intra-mundane planning, hope and
attainment of the future, but as such becomes itself the
communicated, attained future of man.

Christianity presents man then with the *one* question
as to how he really wants to understand himself: whether
as a being active merely *in* the whole, having nothing
to do with the whole as such, although in fact an anticipation of the whole as a symptotic horizon is always the

condition of the possibility of his knowing and action, or whether—as a being receptive-active *of the* whole, having *as such* also to do with this condition of his knowing, acting and hoping and in future-creating activity within the whole—he lets this whole, the absolute future itself come upon him, become as happening for himself. That in the last resort is the sole question presented by Christianity. That this totality of the absolute future cannot really become the object of categorical designation, but remains the ineffable mystery existing in advance of all individual knowledge and every individual action *in regard to* the world and surpassing these, results from the very nature of the totality of the absolute future.

We need only note what are the current concepts of Christian dogmatic theology used to express this thesis that Christianity is the religion of the absolute future, in order to see that Christianity really does understand itself in this way. Absolute future is merely another name for what is really meant by 'God'. For the absolute future, from its very notion, cannot be something to be produced through finite, individual material and categorial combination. On the other hand, as the goal and force of the dynamism of the movement of the world and of man towards the future, as hope bearing these onwards, neither can it be simply the mere empty possible as the *not-yet*-real. It must be the absolute fullness of reality as the moving force of the dynamism of the future. But this absolute future *so* understood is precisely what we call God.

Conversely, from what has been said, two conclusions may be drawn in regard to God. Firstly, he is known precisely *as* the absolute future: he is therefore not an object alongside others, with each of which we have to

deal individually within the system of unlimited co-
ordinates of knowledge and of planning action in regard
to the future, but the very basis of this whole draft of
the future. He is therefore always known simultaneously
when man projects himself towards the future, and even
particularly when he does not give any name to this
whole, but tries to leave it aside. And secondly, God
as absolute future is fundamentally and necessarily the
ineffable mystery, since the original totality of the absolute future towards which man projects himself can never
properly be expressed in its true character coming upon
him as such by means of attributes drawn from intra-
mundane categorial experience. Thus it is, and remains
essentially, mystery, i.e. it is known *as* the essentially
transcendent, of which of course we can say that as a
mystery of infinite fullness it is itself man's absolute
future which communicates itself.

From both peculiarities of the knowledge of God there
follows the possibility of atheism. It is possible firstly
because in regard to his categorial knowledge man can
refuse to submit to the transcendental condition of its
possibility. Secondly because the confrontation with the
fundamental mystery can always be explained as something which is destroyed in its essence if it occurs in
religion, which inevitably has to make use of a categorial
and social instrument. Thirdly because man can naturally
be an atheist in as much as he denies or doubts that God
himself can become his own absolute future and thus can
opt in any event to have nothing to do with him as such.

If then, in Christian terminology, the absolute future
of the world and of man is called God, the event of their
being granted entry to God is called final immediacy of
the world to the God who communicates himself or
immediate vision of God: that is, the immediacy of the

world in its supreme peak of achievement—in man—to the absolute mystery as communicated. What Christianity calls grace is nothing other than God's self-communication as the absolute future in that stage in which the history of its accession and acceptance is still continuing. What is called incarnation of the divine Logos in Jesus Christ means nothing other than that in him objectively and for us this self-communication of God as the absolute future of the world became visible historically in such a way as to become credible as datum, irreversible, and yet conceivable by the categorial experience of man *as such*. But with God, final immediacy to him, with grace and Jesus Christ, is comprehended the whole salvation-reality which Christian faith confesses. But since all these words signify only one thing—namely, that the world possesses an *absolute* future and this truly is salvific, that its becoming has its goal only in the absoluteness of God himself—then it is right for us to say that Christianity is the religion of the absolute future.

3. *Christianity does not promise any intra-mundane future utopia.* It does indeed declare that the decision for the individual human being is realized with his *death*, whether he has made himself open to God's absolute future or not by his actions. But in regard to the collective history of mankind as such, it has as yet no indication of how long this intra-mundane collective history is to last. And in regard to the material *content* of this future, it is likewise neutral. It does not set up any ideals of the future with a particular content, makes no prognoses about these and does not impose on man an obligation in regard to any particular goals of his intra-mundane future. If a future to be planned by man and produced from the resources at his disposal in the world were to be set up as *absolute* future, beyond which there

is nothing and beyond which is to be expected, Christianity would reject the expectation of such a future as utopian ideology.

As ideology, the essence of which consists in assigning a particular, individual reality of the pluralistic world of experience as the absolute fixed point; as utopia, because individually and collectively it is not possible in the long run to confuse a finite intra-mundane future, no matter what its concrete shape may be, with the absolute future or to forbid man to raise questions which go beyond this finite future—which in fact, recognized as finite, he had always already ranged within the wider circle of infinite possibilities. But if no attempt is made to turn an intra-mundane future into such an utopian-ideological absolute, then Christianity is not merely neutral but takes up a *positive* attitude towards any appropriate planning of an intra-mundane future. For it considers precisely this rational, active planned construction of the intra-mundane future the greatest possible liberation of man from the domination of nature, the progressive socialization of men in order to obtain for each the greatest possible scope for freedom as a task imposed together with man's nature as willed by God. This is a task to which man is committed and *in* which he realizes his true religious function, openness of freedom in believing and hoping for the absolute future.

Inasmuch as in Christianity it is only the absolute future of every man that provides the reason of the *absolute* value of every man, a conviction emerges that endows even the intra-mundane concern for the future with its firmest and deepest justification for aiming at an order of society as perfect as possible. If in Christianity love for God and man means *one* commandment and the one realization of authentic Christianity and love for God implies not any kind of ideological complement to the real fulfilment of existence, but the receptive, hopeful openness to the total import of existence, to the absolute future (particularly at the point where this concern no longer permits the active setting up of an intra-mundane kind of future) then with this one commandment and the one fulfilment of existence the innermost dynamism of the intra-mundane alteration of man and of his social situation is also given its true name, without Christianity being on that account in contradiction or competition with an intra-mundane planning of the future. It has itself no intra-mundane future utopia, it permits any realistic planning for the future; it rejects only—but then radically—any ideological utopian future on which the absolute future is confused with an intra-mundane categorical future and in which man's ultimate future is seen in something less than the ineffable, sacred mystery of the absolute God who by grace communicates himself to man and has made the dynamism for this communication the ultimate meaning and motive power of the history of the world and of mankind.

4. *Christianity has nevertheless a real concern for this genuine and appropriate earthly target.* Christianity certainly does not maintain that only *its* supporters could promote this earthly future realistically and with the resources of the whole man, any more than it considers itself alone to be the true bearer of such intra-mundane future goals, any more than it disputes the fact that in its concrete, historical-ecclesial expressions it has frequently been a hindrance to such efforts. For obviously there are human beings who selflessly promote the welfare and social development of man without being perceptibly Christians. Because of its doctrine of the unity of love of

God and love of neighbour, Christianity certainly holds that if someone in *absolute* selflessness lovingly serves man and his dignity, in the affirmation of moral values and imperatives, he affirms God at least implicitly and also effects his salvation before God. But that is far from saying that this sort of thing is possible only in the explicit Christian.

Nevertheless, even as the thematically explicit religion of God as the absolute future, it has a great importance for the intra-mundane society and its aims. By its hope in an absolute future, Christianity protects man from the temptation to apply himself to justified striving after an intra-mundane future with *such* force that every generation is brutally sacrificed to the next and so on, until the future becomes a Moloch to which the real man is sacrificed in favour of a man who is not real but is always still to come. Christianity renders intelligible the fact that even the man who can no longer make any perceptible contribution to the intra-mundane future also maintains his dignity and intangible importance.

Christianity endows working towards ths intra-mundane future with its ultimate, radical seriousness. It explains in its doctrine of the unity of the love of God and love of neighbour that the positive relationship to man is an indispensable, essential factor, an irreplaceable medium for the relationship to God, to him as absolute future (as 'salvation'). But if this human being who is to be loved cannot exist except as the one who projects himself towards his future, then that means that love of God as love of neighbour cannot exist without the will for *this* man and therefore also for his intra-mundane future. Thus this will is not ideologized and not estranged from itself, but simply becomes explicit in its absolute worth and its radically obligatory character.

5. *Christianity as religion of the absolute future will remain.*

a. It will remain. In the long run no one can forbid man to accept his importance. In the history of mankind, the more 'rational' man becomes, the more aware he is of himself and experiences himself in his forever irreplaceable uniqueness, freedom and dignity. The more important and demanding society comes to seem to him, the more will the individual grow in importance. For otherwise society itself would irrevocably become a herd of insignificant creatures. The dignity of society, the radical seriousness of the tasks and demands it imposes, does not diminish but increases the dignity and the radical seriousness which the individual owes to himself and every other individual. From this standpoint, too, he will in future experience more and not less his constant uniqueness. The more man becomes free from the chains of nature, the more he becomes aware of himself, becomes free for himself and in regard to himself. And no economic change and no social system will be able to prevent man from consciously experiencing the limit imposed by death and thus placing himself as a whole in question.

This question cannot be taken away from him: the question of himself as a whole and of the meaning absolutely speaking, not merely of the functional connections of the particular factors of his world and of his existence, but the meaning of the *whole*. He may then explain that he has no answer to this question, he may perhaps *therefore* attempt even now to declare this very question as such to be meaningless. It will continue to present itself: at least it will always be there and remain there as to be ever *again* declared meaningless. And therefore there will always be human beings who have the courage to answer this question with the religion of the absolute future. Such people do not say that they have on *that* plane an answer to the question of the total meaning of existence and the world, the content of which might be presented in intra-mundane terms *alongside* other realities of experience. Rather do they say that the one reason of all plural reality, anticipating everything in itself, from the standpoint of the plurality of these realities of experience, is and remains always and necessarily an incomprehensible mystery.

But they think that it is given to man precisely in this way as man's absolute future and thus can and must be named and expected by him. And this is what they understand by religion. It is not the solution of those questions which arise in this world, to a certain degree functionally, *between* the individual realities in their mutual relationship, but the solution of the question concerned with the *totality* of these plural realities. And since this question will remain, there will also be religion, Christianity, the essence of which consists precisely in not confusing the question of the world with questions *in* the world.

b. This enduring religion will persist too as institutional. Man realizes even his transcendental relationship to a totality of his existence, of his world and of his future —since he has to realize it *also* reflexively—in categorical concepts, in concrete deeds, in social order: in a word, ecclesially. He simply cannot do otherwise. If then there is always the religion of the future, it will always exist also as a social factor. This factor in its historical concreteness will always *also* depend on the profane order of secular society. Since Christianity neither has an idea of this secular society which is binding in a concrete form nor can it prophesy about this, it can also make no forecasts for the future about the concrete form of its own social-ecclesial expression.

But Christianity from the very nature of the case and in its eschatology knows that it will itself be a controversial, even a rejected factor until the advent of the absolute future, no matter how much it is aware of itself as the religion intended for all men. For that very reason it does not expect the ecclesial and the secular society to coincide even materially. It is indeed itself the socially organized community of free belief in the absolute future, of a faith therefore that necessarily rests on the individual decision of each person. Therefore it cannot expect that *in fact* all human beings will belong to it. But since the earthly future of mankind more and more tends towards a social organization of mankind as one and whole and not that of particular nations and historically and regionally limited cultures, so a situation approaches more and more closely in which each will be neighbour to everyone. Hence the fact that in future there will also no longer be any Christian *homogeneous* regional groups and societies. In the historical and social unity of the one mankind, therefore, Christianity will both be everywhere and yet everywhere embrace only a part of mankind—in fact, presumably, only a minority.

Of itself therefore it is interested in living in freedom in a secular society which itself seeks to be in a religious sense pluralistic and creates or permits the possibilities and presuppositions for this, leaving entirely open the question as to how far such a society has to presuppose or create for its permanent existence an intra-mundane homogeneous *Weltanschauung*. A society of the future can sustain such a religious pluralism all the more easily in that it certainly will not want seriously to strive after uniformity as the ideal, as far as an *intra-mundane* ideology is concerned, since that would in fact mean the end of history.

Every theory of an intra-mundane type of future, which as such does not want to abolish history, must therefore necessarily develop a theory of a legitimate intra-mundane and in this sense democratic pluralism. Of itself therefore it cannot escape the task of creating scope within this future for men to exist and to confess themselves to be those who await the absolute future in hope.

CHAPTER 1

The Necessity and Possibility
of Dialogue

Dialogue is an objective necessity of the age.

The absolute necessity for dialogue and co-operation between Christians and Communists stems from two incontestable facts:

1. In this second half of the twentieth century, with the present stockpiles of atomic and thermonuclear bombs, it has become technically possible to annihilate all civilized life on earth. We have come to the tragic and exalting moment in the history of mankind when the human epic which began a million years ago can crumble. If the human race survives, the reason for its survival will not be the simple force of inertia of biological evolution. The race will survive because of a human choice which will have demanded, as Père Teilhard de Chardin said so well, 'the common front of all those who believe that the universe is moving forward, and that it is our task to make it move forward.'[1]

2. The second incontestable fact is that two great conceptions of the world motivate men on this earthly globe, on this ship which sails in space with three billion men aboard and which can at any moment be scuttled by the dissensions of its crew. Hundreds of millions of men find in religious beliefs the meaning of life and death, and the

[1] *Building the Earth*, 1965, p. 121.

very meaning of the history of our race, while other hundreds of millions find that Communism gives a face to the hopes of the earth and a meaning to our history. Thus it is an incontestable fact of our age that the future of man cannot be constructed either against religious believers or without them. Neither can it be constructed against the Communists or without them.

The philosophical problems involved acquire historical dimension in the light of these two enormous facts which dominate our reflections.

It is significant that the necessity of which we speak has been sensed by Catholics as well as by Communists. It was a Catholic theologian who recently wrote: 'For all practical purposes, Marxist humanism nourishes one-third of the world's population today. We cannot condemn out of hand an ideology which sustains so many men and so many nations and which constitutes the hope of so very many of the oppressed and exploited.'[2]

After referring to the appeals for dialogue made by John XXIII, Paul VI and Vatican II, Father González Ruiz describes its perspectives and its limitations. 'From this point on,' he says, 'we can distinguish two specific levels on which Catholic-Marxist dialogue can proceed.

'The first and deepest level touches the religious problem directly. Marxism wages a positive battle against religion because it looks on religion as a brake on human progress. Fundamentally, Marxism is a humanism, and it seeks to elevate man to the highest possible degree of self-realization. Everything which dehumanizes or alienates man has to be suppressed, so that mankind's enormous inherent potentialities might be liberated.

'The essence of man lies in the creation of himself, and

[2] José González Ruiz, s.j., '¿Es posible el diálogo entre católicos y comunistos?' *Juventud Obrera*, No. 91 (February, 1965).

it is only by means of work that this self-creation can be realized . . . considered from this aspect, Marxism's critique of religion is a wholly negative one. Religion takes it for granted that man is a simple executor of plans previously made by God. . . . The Marxist conclusion follows inevitably: in behalf of pure humanism, it must do battle with this religious structure which both denies and interferes with the humanizing role of the creative activity which is proper to man.

'Such is the complexion,' Father González continues, 'of the principal area for dialogue between Catholics and Marxists. It is certain that religion, in and of itself, is inevitably a brake on human progress? . . . It is the urgent duty of Catholics clearly to affirm that the Christian religion . . . does not entail the slightest alienation of man in the purest sense of Marxian humanism. . . . Catholics can in good conscience struggle along with Marxists against all forms of real religious alienation. When we are faced with a concrete instance of religion being conceived or used as a brake on human progress, we can be certain that such religion is not the religion which inspired the whole of the literary riches of the Bible. Treason has been committed against the pure essence of biblical religion.

'The second level on which Catholic-Marxist dialogue can and must proceed is in the area of sociology, which is intimately connected with the properly religious area. The questions presented here include the human meaning of work, the condemnation of the capitalist regime, the suppression of the established classes, the building of socialism. Serious and honest confrontation of ideas is necessary on all these points.'

The very fact that the problem could be presented in this way in 1965 is a 'sign of the times'.

From Anathema to Dialogue

The age of dialogue has definitely succeeded the age of anathema.

For Catholics, this age was inaugurated by John XXIII's great encyclical. The problem of dialogue was placed at the centre of *Ecclesiam Suam* by Paul VI. In France, where the General Secretary of the French Communist Party, Maurice Thorez, had initiated the policy of the 'outstretched hand' in 1936, priests were invited to the *Semaines de la Pensée Marxiste* and participated in them; and Communists were invited to the *Semaine des Intellectuels Catholiques* and participated therein. Four works, by Catholics and Communists in collaboration, have shown the extent of the problem. In Spain, Catholic magazines like *Cuadernos para el Diálogo* and *Serra d'Or* support the idea of dialogue with the Communists which was advanced at the Council itself by the Auxiliary Bishop of Madrid, Guerra Campos. The Communist magazine *Realidad* approaches this problem with the utmost seriousness. After the March, 1963, speech at Bergamo by the General Secretary of the Italian Communist Party, Palmiro Togliatti, whose contribution to the reflections of Marxists on religion was profound, a work of joint Communist-Catholic authorship, similar to the French efforts, marked a new stage of the dialogue in Italy. Magazines such as *Testimonianze* in Florence give serious study to this crucial question. In April, 1965, the powerful association of German Catholics, the *Paulus Gesellschaft*, organized a conference at Salzburg on the theme 'Marxists and Christians Today.'[3] Participants included leading German theologians, French, Italian

[3] See the objective and incisive account of Father Álvarez Bolado, s.j., *Razón y Fé* July, 1965; also the report 'Dialogue between Catholics and Communists,' *Herder Correspondence*, II, 9-10 (September-October, 1965) 325-330.

and Spanish priests, and Communists from five countries. In May, 1965, I was invited by the Catholic Association *Ad Lucem* to the Catholic University of Louvain for the purpose of discussing the significance of Marxian atheism.[4] A debate had taken place in April at the European Centre for Nuclear Research in Geneva, between Christian and Marxist opponents, on the prospects for dialogue between Christians and Marxists. The Soviet periodical *Voprosy Filosofii* devoted an important article in the August, 1965, issue to the 'Dialogue of Catholicism with the Contemporary World.' And in October, 1965, at the invitation of the Department of Philosophy of St Michael's College, University of Toronto, I delivered a lecture on 'The Marxist Christian Dialogue: Possibilities, Problems, Necessity,'[5] which I have elaborated and amplified in the present text. And again, in October 1966, I took part in the first annual conference of the Pierre Teilhard de Chardin Association of Great Britain and delivered a paper on 'The Meaning of History in Marx and Teilhard de Chardin'.

This dialogue and this common quest are not moving forward without arousing a certain amount of uneasiness, resistance and even anger. And it is not unusual to meet with restrictive interpretations and curbs. The narrow and distorted interpretation of the Marxist approach which was presented by Il'icev at Moscow less than two years ago would have made dialogue impossible. But reserve is still more evident in the Church where, even disregarding the unfortunate regressions to the past by *intégristes*, official curbs are many. In May, 1965, for example, the Permanent Commission of the French Episcopate censured the weekly newspaper *Témoignage*

---

[4] Published as 'Marxisme et religion,' Brussels, 1965.
[5] Published in *Continuum*, III, 4 (Winter, 1966), 403-417.

Chrétien for publishing an article by a Communist, an article to which a Dominican had, moreover, replied. These rear-guard actions, however, are incapable of reversing the general forward trend which is inducing Christians to discuss and to plan the future of man with Marxists, and to pose the question of dialogue and alliance without any reservations whatever.

Father González Ruiz, in the article from which we just quoted, distinguished two levels in the dialogue: the level of the conception of man, and the level of politics. The distinction seems legitimate to us; the relating of the two problems strikes us as legitimate too.

For it is not possible, in a discussion of this kind, to put one's conception of man between parentheses and to limit debate to politics. Marxism, like Christianity, does not separate social and political problems from philosophical principles. There is no doubt that we can stand together in warding off immediate dangers, the threat of an atomic war, the crimes of colonialism and torture, while abstracting from one another's conception of the world. But when we face the problem of combining forces for the building of the future, co-operation in mutual trust is going to be possible only if the measures taken and the institutions created—in a word, the *means* adopted—take on meaning and value in terms of conscious *ends* which, even though not identical, at least are acceptable to both parties.

A dialogue so conceived is a demanding dialogue.

Demanding in a double sense: both as to oneself and as to the other. Encounter, when it is not merely a matter of tactics or of chance, must have its source deep within ourselves. A dialogue of this kind demands of each of the participants a fundamental return: for the Christian as for the Marxist, there must be a passing beyond the historical and the transitory so as to pinpoint what is essential and susceptible of no compromise whatever.

During the last few years, this realization has come about on both sides, as each has experienced the need for this return to what is basic.

CHAPTER 2

The Realization of What is Basic
by Christians

Three major events of our age, fabulously expanding man's horizons, have led Christians to distinguish more clearly those elements in their faith which depended upon the historical conditions of Christianity's birth and development from those elements which were essential. The events to which I refer are the dizzying development of science and technology, the proof provided by the socialist revolutions that the capitalist system was not the sole nor even the best form of social relations possible in our time, and the irresistible movement towards national liberation of once-colonial peoples which has created new centres of historical initiative, while revealing sources of human values other than the traditions of the West.

Christians who have responded to these events have done their best to rethink their faith and to live it within the perspectives of the modern world.

On the level of knowledge, they have been introduced to the problem of 'demythologizing' the Christian message and, in a more general way, to the problem of the relationship of religion and science.

On the level of action, they have been introduced to the problem of the relations of the Christian with the world, with the society of his time.

From Anathema to Dialogue

A. THE CHRISTIAN, MYTH AND SCIENCE

a) Since 1941, the problem of 'demythologizing' has been presented in new terms by the Protestant theologian Rudolf Bultmann and his contrasting of Christian 'kerygma' and myth.

Bultmann starts from the consciousness of conflict between contemporary scientific thought and the mythology in which the Christian message has traditionally been wrapped. Bultmann's problem is this: How deliver what is essential in the 'kerygma' (Christian preaching) from the mythical coating which links the basic call to an outdated conception of the world?

Bultmann's theology is radically distinct from the exegesis of the liberals. The liberal school was inclined to discard as mythical all the images which surrounded what was essential in the Gospel, while strictly limiting the essential to a body of immanent truths and values.

Bultmann is in opposition to the liberals on two points. The esssential point of opposition is his view of the message (the 'kerygma') as an act of God summoning us, confronting us, through the revelation of Christ, with a divine event; although it comes 'from without', this event also judges us and saves us by calling us to begin a new future. Wholly unlike the theology of the liberals, which did away with transcendence, Bultmann's theology tends to acknowledge transcendence in its most exalted form, as a dramatic invasion of the divine into the history of man. The second fundamental difference between Bultmann and liberal exegesis lies in the conception of myth and the role of myth. It is not Bultmann's purpose to eliminate the mythological, but to give it an existential interpretation as myth instead.

According to Bultmann, the biblical and evangelical

message is not an ideology, nor is it bound to any theoretical conception of the world, God, and their relations, or to any philosophy. It is a strictly personal message. It is like an intimate dialogue of God's call and man's response. It creates within our lives the dimension of responsibility.

The believer is responsible for his faith. God demands that he decide. The important thing about the event of the Cross, for example, is not its historical, objective reality as a fact of the past, one which could have occurred even if no witnesses had ever given a meaning to it or transformed their lives in terms of their encounter with it. The important thing is the act by which the believer acknowledges, deep within himself, the call of God.

Myth, then, is the form in which the invasion of the transcendent into man's life is expressed in the language of the imagination and in the terms of each epoch's conception of the world. As it recounts in imaged and symbolic form how and why a particular event has come about, myth bestows meaning on the world and on human existence. In this way, it presents man with a model, an exemplary manner of being and of acting. Its role in the developing construction of man is enormous, simply because it makes present and accessible at every stage in history and culture everything which has not been subjected to the rational ordering of the world.

But the myth to which we have reference is of no value by itself. It takes on value only through the decision of the believer, for whom symbol has become openness to transcendence.

Naturally, the images and forms in which myth is expressed bear the imprint of the age which saw its birth. Thus, the Christian message was translated into the inadequate language of the ideologies, myths and philosophies of the ancient world. The ascension of Christ was expressed in the language of Ptolemy; transcendence was thought of as extension in space; creation was sometimes thought of on the Greek model of demiurgy, sometimes on the Gnostic model, sometimes on the model of empirical causality, and sometimes as an upheaval *ex nihilo*; miracles were ascribed to the workings of hidden forces. Yet all this is simply the transposition, on archaic cultural levels, of one basic message: God's judgment on man and God's salvation of man by manifesting himself to man on the Cross. It is this faith alone which reveals to man how profound, both as gift and as freedom, existence is.

For Bultmann, this actual encounter with a God who is personal through his freely given love remains a 'scandal': openness to the future which lies ahead implies that man will not rely solely on his own works, but will receive, if he is to be saved, the power of the Other. 'Faith,' writes Bultmann, 'as the liberation of man in his own regard, as openness to the future, is only possible under the outward manifestations of a faith in the love of God.'[1] This faith frees us by elevating us to the authentic existence in which we love men with the freely given love with which God loves us. And this is salvation, our final end. Rather than something to be thought of under the mythological form of a future life, it is an actual eschatological achievement, *hic et nunc*. Man becomes a person by his decision to go out of himself and answer the summons of God served on him by his neighbour.

One of the specific features of Bultmann's apologetic is the attempt to grasp the point at which the supernatural is infused into man, and in terms of Heideggerian existen-

[1] *Cf.* 'New Testament and Mythology,' *Kerygma and Myth*, vol. I, London, 1953, p. 32.

tial categories: the message is rather like an answer to a question, to an expectation written within us.

Bultmann's apologetic begins to make the coming of God acceptable to modern man.

The problem, therefore, has been presented. Today, it is presented to all believers.

Divino afflante Spiritu, Pope Pius's XII's encyclical of September 30, 1943, approaches the problem of demythologizing from the viewpoints of tradition, magisterium, and dogma.

In a book devoted to Bultmann's theology, L. Malevez underlines the essential aspect of the question: 'Concern for a formulation of the Christian message which will make it easier for modern man to understand: here too, Bultmann confronts the theologian with a task which he cannot evade.'[2]

Ultimately, Père Malevez rejects Bultmann's conception because of his own view that the believer is deprived of the active presence of the Saviour when the idea of a 'non-phenomenal intervention of God in nature and in history'[3] is excluded on principle. In order to preserve this possibility, Père Malevez draws a distinction between 'philosophical reason' which articulates this exclusion and 'scientific reasoning' which abstracts from it. But may this not be a return to the dangerous attempt to place God inside the provisional gaps of science, an attempt which has consistently led theology into useless and retreating battles against science?

For the problem of the necessary reinterpretation of dogma is still with us.

Shortly after the appearance of the encyclical *Divino*

[2] L. Malevez, s.j., *The Christian Message and Myth*, Westminster, Maryland, 1958, p. 119.
[3] *ibid.*, p. 131.

afflante Spiritu, Henri de Bouillard, s.j., in *Conversion et Grâce chez Saint Thomas d'Aquin*, offered another treatment of the distinction between the permanent affirmation of the Christian message and the presentations of it which have successively been offered, presentations which develop along with the thought and culture of men in every age. Some theologians reacted to this attempt by denouncing a latent agnosticism which they detected in it.

Even more violent were the reactions of the partisans of theological immobility in March, 1963, when the general public was introduced to the problem of demythologizing by the appearance of a small book by the Anglican Bishop John A. T. Robinson, *Honest to God*—a book which sold a million copies in several months.

The book's success is apparently due to two principal reasons:

1. Bishop Robinson separates the problem of demythologizing from the Bultmannian existentialist interpretations which had given it an esoteric cast. Robinson sees the problem as one of stripping away from the Christian message everything which is mythical: everything which has meaning only in terms of an insufficiently rationalized conception of the world.

2. Robinson's conception of the relationship between God and the world is in accord with the aspirations of millions of believers today. We do not come to God by turning away from the world. We come to God by 'a deeper immersion in existence'.[4] God is incarnate in the Other: ' "The 'beyond' [is] *in the midst of our life,*" the

---

[4] *Honest to God*, SCM Press, London, 1963, p. 47 (quoting Kierkegaard).

holy *in* the common.'[5] No longer is the relationship between God and the world a relationship of alternatives:
'either God *or* the world'. Now it is a dialectical relationship: 'God *in* the world'. 'This is the essence of the
religious perversion, when worship becomes a realm into
which to withdraw from the world to "be with God"—
even if it is only in order to receive strength to go back
into it.'[6]

Seen in this perspective, transcendence is no longer an
attribute of God but a dimension of man, a dimension of
our experience and our acts. It is what is specifically
human in man, as against what is animal in him, and
what is alienated.

How far can demythologizing and de-alienation go
before religion itself is brought into question? The
answer is not one which should be given by an unbeliever,
and even if it were, it is not on the answer to questions of
this kind that the fruitfulness of dialogue and Christian-
Communist collaboration depends.

The profundity of such dialogue and collaboration is
decisively conditioned on the effort made by each, and
each in his own way, to elicit the fundamental from what
gives meaning and value to our lives—from Christianity
for some, from Marxism for others—and then, after we
have eliminated the accidental and the contingent, to see
if there is an overlap of enough that is fundamental to
enable us to construct together, and without hidden
motives, the common city and the future of the man
who lacks none of his dimensions, the 'total' man, as
Marx put it, the 'entire' man, in Père Teilhard's expression.

Our reference to the Christian reflection on what is

[5] *ibid.*, p. 86.
[6] *ibid.*, pp. 86-87.

basic can then be seen simply as an effort to discern the common movement which bears it onward.

The actual movement has been defined with considerable clarity by Father González.[7] He speaks of 'the Catholic temptation'. Catholicism is the heir of Greco-Latin culture and its love of myth. As Father González sees it, there is an habitual temptation in the Mediterranean world to tame the transcendent by clear and concrete forms—those of image and myth.

In the face of critical attacks which, even from the time of Xenophanes and Euripides, had regularly denounced the anthropomorphic relativism of classical myths, the Catholic Church has tended to be reticent regarding the painful problems of demythologizing. 'If we want to be honest,' Father Ruiz writes, 'we must acknowledge the fact . . . that myths are both beautiful and convenient, and that they serve to maintain the cohesiveness of the great socio-political constructs in which the Mediterranean world has been caught up since the time of the Roman Empire, then during medieval Christendom, and up to the great colonialist undertaking of the modern age.'

There is also what Father González calls 'the Protestant temptation'. This seeks to reduce to the absolute minimum the transcendence, ultimately a disincarnate one, of a God who is totally 'other', and to consider all of the floridly Oriental literature of the Bible as a purely expressive form. This too has a grandeur of its own and a purifying strength.

Father González concludes: 'Every effort to escape from this dialectical tension—whether it be to the right,

[7] José González Ruiz, s.j., 'El cristianismo y el demitologismo,' *Revista de Occidente*, February, 1965.

by settling into myth, or to the left, by eliminating myth once and for all—is a grievous sin of mediocrity committed against the development and evolution of a faith and hope whose sights are set on an *eschaton* present at the very centre of the frontiers of history.'

b) *The problem of the relationship of religion and science*, rather than being presented merely under the aspect of demythologizing, is also presented in a more general way. No one has treated it with greater thoroughness than Père Teilhard de Chardin, s.j.

In every age, the scientific conception of the world has an impact on the way men think about God and about their own job in the world. This is why every period of great scientific progress, by changing the general view of the world, has led to great religious crises. With this historical finding as a point of departure, Père Teilhard presents the problem of an up-to-date formulation of the Christian faith which takes account of the changes which have occurred in the world.

If this new formulation of the faith is to be contemporary with twentieth-century man, it must, according to Père Teilhard, comply with three requirements:

1. The elimination from theology of all that is still linked to an archaic conception of the world. Revelation occurred at a time when the cosmos was thought of as a finite and static whole.

2. The definition of the relationship possible between God and the world in a world which is conceived as a living organic totality, in ceaseless evolution and creation.

3. The elaboration of a theology which fully recognizes the value of work and of human effort, of scientific research as well as technical invention.

A passage from Teilhard on original sin, in 'Christo-

41

logie et Evolution', an article written in 1933, provides a clear-cut example of his working approach to this three-fold requirement:

'When we try to live and to think Christianity with the whole of our modern souls, the first resistance encountered always arises from original sin. This is true, first of all, for the research worker. He finds in the traditional presentation of the Fall a decisive obstacle to all progress, taken as a broad perspective on the world. All things considered, it is only because we are trying to save the letter of the story of the Fault that we go on defending the actual reality of the first couple. . . . But . . . here is something more serious still. Not only must history, so as to accept Adam and Eve, be strangled, in a quite artificial way, on the level of the appearance of man, but—in a more immediately vital area, that of belief—the expansion of our religion is constantly stifled by the present formulation of the doctrine of original sin. It clips the wings of our expectations and inexorably leads us back into the shadows of reparation and expiation.

'. . . Original sin, as still imaginatively presented today, is the tight collar which strangles our minds and hearts. . . . If the dogma of original sin binds and weakens us, the simple reason is that it represents, in its present form, the survival of the static views which have become outdated in our now-evolutionist way of thinking. The idea of the Fall is, after all, basically nothing but an attempt to explain evil in a deterministic universe. . . . In point of fact, Christianity, notwithstanding the subtle distinctions of the theologians, developed under the dominant impression that all the evil around us stemmed from an initial fault. Dogmatically, we live in the atmosphere of a universe whose principal business was reparation and expiation. . . . For a variety of reasons, scientific, moral and religious, the classic formulation of the Fall has ceased to be anything other than a yoke and a verbal affirmation which nourishes neither our minds nor our hearts.'

After stressing the conservative implications of this conception of original sin and the attitudes of expiation and resignation which flow from it, Père Teilhard continues:

'There has been entirely too much talk about lambs. I would like to see the lions a bit more. Too much sweetness, and not enough strength. This is how I sum up symbolically my observations and my thesis on the question of readaptation of evangelical doctrine to the modern world.'

Père Teilhard spells out the practical consequences of the modern conception of the world.

'We Christians are pleased to think that, if so many Gentiles remain apart from the faith, the reason is that the ideal which is preached to them is too perfect and too difficult. This is an illusion. Souls have ever been fascinated by the nobly difficult. Witness, in our own day, the advance of Communism, in the midst of martyrs. . . . As a matter of fact, the most outstanding unbelievers I know would think they were slipping from their moral ideal if they were to take steps towards conversion.'

Looking for means of 'readapting' the Church to the new world, Père Teilhard added:

'We can answer in one word: by becoming, for God, the pillars of evolution. Until now, the Christian has been brought up under the impression that he had to leave all in order to attain God. What he is now discovering is that he cannot be saved except through and as an **extension of the universe.** . . .

43

'In the past, adoration was the preference of God to things by referring them to him and by sacrificing them to him. Adoration has now become our devotion, body and soul, to the creative act by associating ourselves with it for the fulfilment of the world through effort and research.

'. . . Detachment, in the past, meant dissociating oneself from things and taking from them only the barest minimum. Detachment will more and more become the progressive superseding of all truth and beauty by the strength of the love we bring to them.

'Resignation, in the past, could mean the passive acceptance of present conditions in the universe. Resignation now will be permitted only to those who struggle feebly between the hands of the angel.'

Père Teilhard concluded: 'This evangelism has about it no more of the fragrance of opium we have been so bitterly (and with some justification) criticized for spreading among the masses.'

I think that we have here the key to the apologetic of Père Teilhard de Chardin.

It seems that science and religion are, for Père Teilhard, complementary readings of the world. It is possible to take an analytical path which goes right back to the elements, and it is also possible to live in harmony with the movement of synthesis and ascent. 'Matter and spirit,' writes Teilhard, 'are not opposed like two things or two natures, but like two directions taken by evolution within the world.' There is, on the one hand, the liberation of energy, and, on the other, the process of unification. The very advance of science, grasped in its basic unity and direction, suggests the need of this ascent and inspires love for it. 'A religion of earth is now being formed in exchange for the religion of heaven. This, basically, is the problem which confronts us, in all its seriousness but in all its promise too.'

'From beneath the exegetical difficulties of detail, a basic religious antinomy thus emerged, the very antinomy which was obscurely implied in the Galileo controversy. Once the universe had been recognized as being in movement, a kind of divinity, wholly immanent in the world, tended gradually to be substituted in the human consciousness for the transcendent Christian God. . . . This is the mortal danger with which the Catholic Church in our age sees herself more and more menaced every day.'

For Teilhard, the problem is the integration of this general trend of mankind into Christianity. He asserts 'the right and the dignity of saying to a humanist or Marxist colleague: *Plus et ego . . .*'

There can be no doubt that this conversion of the Church to the hopes of the earth demands bold initiative: 'To immerse oneself so as to emerge and to lift up. To participate so as to sublimate. This is the very law of the Incarnation. One day, a thousand years ago, the popes said farewell to the Roman Empire and decided "to go over to the barbarians".' May not a similar and even more profound gesture be expected today?

'In my opinion, the world will not be converted to the heavenly promises of Christianity unless Christianity has previously been converted (so as to divinize them) to the promises of the earth.'

Père Teilhard never puts faith in the hereafter in opposition to the earthly combat. 'Taken by itself, faith in the world is not sufficient to move the earth forward. But is it perfectly certain that, taken by itself, the Christian faith, as explained in the past, is still sufficient to lift the world up to the Summit?' And he went so far as to add: 'The synthesis of the [Christian] God of the Above and the [Marxist] God of the Ahead: this is the only God whom we shall in the future be able to adore in spirit and in truth.'

The problem of the whole man has possibly never been so boldly presented, even if insufficient importance is given to negation in his construction of the world.

Seen in this perspective, Christianity does not rule out but actually implies militant effort turned towards the future and its construction. 'As men, it is our duty to act as if there were no limits to our power. Having become, by existence, collaborators in a creation which is developing within us in such a way as will very likely lead us to an end (even earthly) which is far more exalted and far off than we think, we must help God with all our strength and so work with matter as if our salvation depended on our industry alone.'

This conception of Christianity as a 'religion of action' and this revaluation of the world answer not only to the problem of the relationship of religion and science but also to the problem of the relations between Christianity and society.

B. THE CHRISTIAN, SOCIETY AND
   ITS FUTURE

A Christianity which is in harmony with the world rather than at odds with it and turned away from it as from a blemish is not a twentieth-century innovation. Side-by-side with the tradition of *The Imitation of Christ*, there is a tradition of Christian humanism in the Catholic Church. The latter has received emphasis whenever man has made a decisive advance towards mastery of nature, society and his own future. During the Renaissance,

Cardinal Bellarmine wrote *The Mind's Ascent to God by a Ladder of Created Things.* The extraordinary renaissance of this twentieth century of ours has brought such a state of mind back to life, and not simply for a small elite of humanists but for great masses of mankind.

Among Protestants, the transition from Karl Barth's *Commentary on the Epistle to the Romans* to his *The Humanity of God,* or the brilliant success of Robinson's book, is also symptomatic of this development.

In Catholic thought, there are a number of currents, the most significant of which is Teilhardism, which are moving forward in the same direction. It is noteworthy that Pope John XXIII, from the very beginning of *Pacem in terris,* insisted not on man's nothingness but on his power. The encyclical opens with the affirmation that 'God created man with intelligence and freedom . . . making him lord of creation'. The Pope elected to quote these verses from Psalm 8: 'You have made him little less than the angels, and crowned him with glory and honour. You have given him rule over the works of your hands, putting all things under his feet.' The Council's Schema 13, on the Church's orientation before the modern world, seems vivified by the same spirit.

In thus putting the accent on human initiative, many Christians have experienced the return to what is basic as a return to primitive Christianity. Passing over the many centuries of the Church's 'Constantinian' tradition (a tradition constituted by close connections with the ruling classes and the established power, and by the assimilation of Greco-Latin ideologies with their hierarchical conceptions of the world), many Christians today are attempting to rediscover the apocalyptic tradition of primitive Christianity, the tradition of an age when Christianity was a slaves' religion, a protest, however weak, against the established order, and a hope for the coming of the Kingdom on earth as in heaven, when Christianity had not yet become an ideology of imperial justification and of resignation.

The whole history of the Church is criss-crossed by this internal dialectic, this inherent opposition between the Constantinian tradition, with its accent on sin and its office of justifying the State and ruling classes—themselves seen as providential and legitimate instruments for the guidance of men incapable of freedom—and the apocalyptic tradition (a tradition whose vigour revives whenever the masses become aware of their power), with its accent on the affirmation that the Man-God has triumphed over sin and its occasional effort to translate the apocalypse into history. The Constantinian tradition has consecrated all class domination—slavery, serfdom, the salary system—and has associated the Church with itself. The apocalyptic tradition gave life to the rebellions of John Hus as well as the more recent colonial heresies. It is quite possible that the underlying orientation of the movement towards *aggiornamento*, under pressure exerted by the transformation of the conditions of human existence in the twentieth century, is that the apocalyptic is gaining ground over the Constantinian.

This historical exigency has led some of the greatest theologians of our times—perhaps without their being fully aware of it—forcefully to recapture what is specifically Christian from those earlier ideologies which had been assimilated by Christianity when it became a syncretistic religion.

As conceived by classical Greek humanism, the world is a cosmos: an organic whole which is subject to the laws of reason and of beauty; man is integrated into nature and into the city as one of its organs or fragments.

With Christianity, a new status for man in regard to the world appeared, one which constituted a radical departure from that of Greek humanism. Existence, for man, is no longer a matter of being inserted into the Whole of the cosmos as one of its fragments. For man to exist has now become the liberation from his nature and his past, by the divine grace revealed in Christ, liberation for a life which consists in free decisions. As of this moment, authentic 'history' has become possible: to the timeless contemplation of the eternal laws of the cosmos, there succeeds an unfolding of life in time, where the past is the *locus* of sin, where the future which lies always before us is the *locus* of grace, and where the present is the time for decision, the time for rejection or acceptance of the divine call.

During the Salzburg colloquy on 'Marxists and Christians Today,' on May 1, 1965, in reply to my definitions of Marxist humanism as the methodology of historical initiative for the realization of the total man, Father Karl Rahner s.j., striking boldly at the heart of the problem, stated that the experience of God is required for an integral humanism. Making explicit the specifically Christian aspect of this experience of God, he defined Christianity as 'the religion of the absolute future'. Far from being a sacralization of the historical present, Christianity teaches us to understand everything on the basis of what is in process of arrival.

According to Father Rahner, an authentically human history, one made up of free decisions, and a truly human progress are possible only through the impulse given to every human project by the transcendent existence of an absolute plenitude. It is only for this reason that man, plunged into history, is able at every moment to sum up history's meaning and to promote its eclipse of itself. This active and demanding presence of the absolute future is in everyone. It is this which makes atheism possible. Atheism results when man fails to recognize his God in this appeal and confuses the absolute future with one of his concrete futures, with what he can project of his own future at any given moment in history.

On the other hand, when God is recognized in this absolute future whose ascendancy over history becomes apparent as the irreversible destiny of any sincere humanism, we see the three fundamental Christian dogmas in their true light: the dogma of the total consummation of the world in God (beatific vision), the dogma that this very anticipation is already present in God and constitutes the principle of all human creation (grace), and the dogma of the Incarnation which makes of the Christian faith the highest affirmation of man and the very antithesis of a mythology of evasion.

The first and most important consequence of this theology of the absolute future is that the Christian faith cannot conflict with any historical orderings for the construction of the earthly city, at least to the extent that they are authentically human.

From then on, the criterion of a social order's value remains purely immanent: to what extent does it create the conditions in which man can develop in a human way? Christianity stimulates historical creativity by revealing the transitory character of every historical present, and fully participates in man's development since it is through this total development that man can encounter God. An attitude like this surely entitles us to place the dialogue on a new and higher plane. It is at this level that Father González Ruiz, in the periodical put out by the Young Catholic Workers of Spain, poses the question: 'Socialism brings to the world a greater measure of justice than the old social structures. The human meaning of work, the suppression of class distinctions, the building of socialism . . . a serious and honest confrontation of ideas on all these points is in order.'

At the same time, Father Rahner added, Christianity, by asserting an essential difference between every human project, be it individual or collective, and the absolute future, avoids the temptation of brutally sacrificing each generation in favour of the next succeeding and of thus 'making of the future a Moloch to which the real man is sacrificed in favour of a man who is not real but is always still to come'.

Finally, Christianity, as the religion of the absolute future, will remain throughout all the stages of history: since no human project can be equal to the absolute plenitude for which every man hopes, there will always be men to affirm the reality of an absolute future which exceeds whatever may be realized.

It was on the basis of positions such as these that Father J. B. Metz, another theologian at the Salzburg Colloquy, asked the Marxists three questions about their conception of man and his future:

1. Will the realization of the total man give the final answer to man's questions, or will man, when fully developed, be still more the questioner, more capable still of an ever-expanding future? Will the future be filled with questions which exceed and transcend our projects and our tentative notions of the future? This would in no way contradict the autonomy of the human race since it is this openness to the future which constitutes the very essence of man.

2. Where can a critical philosophy, such as Marxism, derive the negative capability which permits it to be dissatisfied with given historical situation? Does it not come precisely from a reality which lies both behind and before the question, indeed contains the question, and which inspires in man both the nostalgia for 'more-being' and the confidence in a future which is always in excess of anything that can be identified with any human project?

3. How, at the very heart of an alienated society—and until now there has been no other kind—can we have any confidence in the impression of a promised future of fullness, when this future itself is nothing but our project as alienated men, when this future is not a redemptive future which, on its own initiative, comes towards us without ceasing? Our future can be this full openness only through the intimate experience of the *Deus semper major* who always exceeds our projects and our plans and who comes to our level in life, to the very heart of our freedom, our power and our effort to transform the world.

Father Metz's questions, like Father Rahner's theses, essentially tend to show that the Marxists' tension towards the future itself contains, though without their realizing it, the question which God asks us and Christianity answers. As they see it, Marxism simply cannot evade the Christian question, for at the very heart of a humanism which strives to be integral the question of the future of man gives birth to the question of the future of God.

It is precisely this question which Père Georges Cottier, o.p., has posed: 'How does man acquire this dimension of infinity? Is its meaning exhausted by the indefinite dialectical process of man's surpassing of himself on the level and within the limits of his own history? This awareness of incompleteness . . . may this not be the mark of man's openness to a transcendent ontological infinite?'

Père Cottier is right in saying that 'these are great questions, which human thought must not fail to ask'.

We can understand these questions because they are asked in the language of our time. Up to this point, we have done our best to summarize, in as objective a manner as possible and without yet entering into discussion of them, the reflections of Catholic or Protestant theologians on a number of problems. These have included the problems of demythologizing and of the relationship of faith and science, and the problems connected with man's future and with the relationship of faith to the building of that future. The efforts of these theologians have made a true dialogue possible. Rather than turning us away from them, their questions have stimulated our clearest thinking and our most militant action.

A theology which is frantically bound to conceptions of the world which have been outdated for ten or twenty centuries has no meaning for us, if indeed for anyone. The theologian of a degenerate Scholasticism is no contemporary of ours, nor do we even share a common language.

A theology bound to the justification of established disorder, to the ruling classes and their privileges, also makes dialogue impossible. Relations with it can only occur on the level of our political struggle against the forces of the past with which it makes common cause.

The touchstone of the vitality of Christian teaching is its attitude to the progress of science and to the development of a new society.

When the Church transforms itself into a machine for the production of orthodoxy and resignation, it produces with even greater efficiency today's atheism and anger.

An Uruguayan Jesuit, Father Segundo, writing in 1962 about 'the future of Christianity in Latin America', made an analysis of the new conditions of Christian life: the destruction of closed societies, the discovery by Christians of their minority status in the world and their consequent need to adapt to a pluralistic society, the awareness of the compromises made by the Church and her alliances with power and oppression. The result has been the remarkable rapidity of the process of de-christianization: 'Once the Christian-making machine—the social pressure of closed Christian societies, of Christian schools, etc.—stopped in Latin America, there was absolutely nothing left. . . . The Christians in Brazil became adherents of spiritism because their Christendom had been a product of this Christian-making machine.' And yet baptisms continue even there, as by routine, so as to preserve the appearance of an official Christendom, though it is empty as a secularized cathedral.

Father Segundo gives several striking examples, such as the following: 'Everyone is aware that in Brazil, for example, certain Catholic universities are supported by industrialists. When an industrialist learns that a portion of the Church's social doctrine which can be interpreted as a criticism of capitalism is being said at the university, he will telephone the rector: "Excuse me, but the support I had been giving to the university will no longer be available . . .".' Father Segundo's conclusion from such examples is: 'In Latin America, concern for the preservation of Catholic institutions by any and every possible means has compromised Christianity far more than it has in Europe, and has corrupted the very words in which Christianity must be proclaimed, must be preached. And we have no other words.'

The efforts of the theologians we have been speaking about show that there may be other words after all. They show that a pastoral theology of witness and dialogue can follow upon an earlier pastoral theology of authority, anathema and constraint. When John XXIII speaks about war and peace, when Père Teilhard or Père Dubarle speaks about science, when Father González Ruiz or Father Rahner speaks about the future, they speak a language which can reach even us, can force us to ask questions, can stimulate intellectual rivalry and mutual enrichment. It is a language which not only makes dialogue possible but also makes it possible to have real co-operation in the building of a common future that our times demand.

An objection, of course, crops up, one which is *intégriste* in origin. It goes as follows: Christians who enter into dialogue are playing a fool's game—Communists accept dialogue when they are out of power and turn it down when they are in. Why should Christians take the step from anathema to dialogue when it is their own willingness which will enable Communists to move on from dialogue to persecution?

The question is both wrong-headed and improper, but it must be answered.

For those, first, who use the question as an anti-Soviet and anti-Communist weapon, it is useful to recall three facts of history regarding religion in the Soviet Union.

1. Before the October Socialist Revolution, there was a state religion in Russia. It was the religion of the Ortho-

dox Church and it was closely linked to the feudal and czarist regime of exploitation and oppression. The links were those of a gilded vassalage, with all the compromises, all the servility, and all the corruption which that suggests. Just as in the France of the *ancien régime,* the Church was but an aspect of the State. And in Russia, this brought with it the persecution of all other churches and religions, whether Uniate or Protestant, Jewish or Moslem.

2. During the early years of the Revolution, the old-line official Church, long since domesticated by the monarchy and the privileged classes, gave, by and large, political and often military support to counter-revolutionary movements. Those who fell in the ranks of the feudal armies, or intervening foreign allies, could be considered as martyrs for the faith.

3. At the present time, the situation can be summoned up as follows—provided one knows how to make the necessary allowances for the exaggerations, indeed the downright lies, of a propaganda which seeks to throw the cloak of religion over the political ends of an anti-Soviet crusade: it would appear that the religious problem has been resolved to the satisfaction neither of the Christians nor of the Marxists. Although it is false that believers are 'persecuted', news from the Soviet Union does suggest that bureaucratic vexation exists—even though it is contrary to the fundamental principles of the Soviet regime, and is, as a result, frequently denounced and censured by higher authority. It remains true that such practices continue, on the local level at least. It also remains true that they are not always combatted as vigorously as principles demand, but this is due to a narrow, feeble interpretation of the Marxist conception of religion and to a basic failure to grasp the reality

of the religious fact—something which has been apparent even in official texts, which we have had occasion publicly to criticize. If we wish to be completely objective, we shall have to acknowledge, on the one hand, that the *de facto* political activity of sects like the 'Jehovah's Witnesses' does lead to a kind of sabotage which justifies a certain vigilance, and, on the other hand, that the correction of exaggerations and errors continues on the theoretical level itself.

Another historical experience can also give Catholics some cause for reflection on the future of their Church in a socialist regime. I refer to the Polish experience.

Without drawing any inference either on the conduct of the Catholic Church in Poland or on the religious policy of the Polish State, we cannot help but be impressed by a single bare fact: in 1937, there were 40 bishops, 11,000 priests, and 15,000 men and women religious in Poland; in Poland in 1965, there are 70 bishops, 16,000 priests, and 30,000 men and women religious. According to statistics assembled by Professor Maïka of the Catholic University of Lublin, 80 per cent of the population are practising Catholics. The Catholic press publishes a number of periodicals. To cite but one example, the weekly newspaper of the Diocese of Katowice has a circulation of 80,000.

Who can honestly speak of persecution or of a 'Christianity of silence'?

What is taking place actually suggests that socialism has brought about a 'boom' in Catholicism! A boom which seems to owe nothing to any particular openness on the part of the Polish hierarchy, whose representatives at the Council made no reputation for boldness, nor to a spiritual renewal of Polish Catholicism, whose hierarchical expression appears conservative rather than forward-looking (at Christmas, 1964, Cardinal Wyszinski came out rather harshly with a reminder, for the benefit of the Catholic magazine *Wiench* [*The Bond*]—whose point of view is roughly equivalent to that of the French monthly *Esprit*—that Catholic intellectuals have no active voice in the affairs of the Church).

What has come about is a simple sociological phenomenon: before the War, the Catholic Church was closely linked with the State and with the propertied classes; the socialist regime, by making compromises of this sort impossible, has rooted out an underlying cause of discredit and disaffection in regard to the Church. This is simply the counterproof of the historical experience in Latin America as described by Father Segundo.

Today there is an increasing amount of reflection on these experiences by thinking Christians.

Speaking in Rome, at the time of the Council, on 'Religious Liberty in the New Testament', Father González Ruiz, a *peritus,* seemed to draw the lessons from this twofold historical proof: 'A Church which is bound up with the State—a Church which demands or accepts a privileged position in society, such as an academic monopoly—places limitations on her religious liberty and on her power of denunciation. . . . Thus there comes about . . . the gradual absorption of the prophetic by the cultual . . and the inflation of the cultual defiles the Church by blurring what is deepest in her religious identity: the prophetic element.'

Now that these prejudicial objections have been disposed of, it is possible to enquire of the Marxists as we have been enquiring of the Christians. How have they been led, during the last ten years in particular—thanks to the collective examination of conscience encouraged by the Twentieth Congress of the Communist Party of the

Soviet Union (both by the prospects for the future which it introduced and by the sorrowful revelations of the past which it invited Communists all over the world to judge) —to rethink their conception of the world and their methods for meeting the challenge of the problems posed by our age?

CHAPTER 3

The Realization of What is Basic by Marxists

It is remarkable that the return to the basic should have begun, for Marxist philosophers as well as for Christians, with a fresh study of the sources in an effort to discover the specifically Marxist elements in the materialism of their doctrine, the radically new contribution of Marx to philosophy.

This development in research brings us to the very heart of our study, for the simple reason that the major portion of the theoretical misunderstandings between Christians and Marxists result from the great confusion about the word 'materialism'.

Marxism's specific difference from all earlier forms of materialism lies in the fact that Marxism takes as its point of departure the *creative act of man*.

Marx emphasizes this radical difference in his 'Theses on Feuerbach'; 'The chief defect of all materialism up to now (including Feuerbach's) is that the object, reality, what we apprehend through our senses, is understood only in the form of the *object* or *contemplation*; but not as *sensuous human activity*, as *practice*; not subjectively.'[1]
It is remarkable that in this text, generally considered—

[1] In Karl Marx and Friedrich Engels, *The German Ideology*, New York, 1947, p. 197.

and with good reason—to be the birth certificate of Marxist philosophy, seven of the eleven theses are directly devoted to identifying the various aspects of the creative act of man:

—the *active* side of knowledge,

—the criterion of *practice*, the sole criterion of truth,

—the definition of the role of philosophy as the *transformation* of the world.

This Faustian primacy of action, in Marx, betrays the Fichtean and Hegelian origins of his philosophy. 'The outstanding achievement of Hegel's *Phenomenology*,' Marx wrote in 1844, '. . . is that he conceives objective man (true, because real man) as the results of his own labour.'[2] This becomes the keystone of his conception of socialism: 'For the socialist, everything that is called universal history is simply the generation of man by human work.'

This is not a conception which was limited to the works of Marx's youth. It is a key idea which dominates the thought and struggles of Marx, of Engels, and of Lenin too.

In *Dialectics of Nature*, Engels will reiterate and will demonstrate that 'work has created man himself'.

In *Capital*, Marx distinguishes human work from that of the animals by emphasizing the importance of the creative action of ends, of project: 'At the end of every labour-process, we get a result that already existed in the imagination of the labourer at its commencement. He not only effects a change of form in the material on which he works, but he also realizes a purpose of his own that

---

[2] 'Critique of Hegel's Dialectic and General Philosophy,' *Karl Marx: Early Writings* (Bottomore, tr. and ed.), London, 1963, p. 202.

gives the law to his *modus operandi*, and to which he must subordinate his will.'[3]

In 'The Eighteenth Brumaire of Louis Bonaparte', Marx says once again that 'men make their own history'.

How, in spite of such insistence, has it been possible to ascribe to Marx a supposed 'economic determinism' which is so contrary to the basic spirit of his doctrine?

The reason for this, it seems to me, is that Marx's analysis of the creative act of human work is a materialist's analysis. Unlike the idealist philosophers, Marx does not reduce human activity to spiritual activity. His essential discovery—a materialist conception of human work as a creative act—consisted in his realization that a bond exists between the act of thinking and the whole of social practice, and in his consequent forging of a new critical method which seeks outside of thought itself the sources and conditions of thought and the experimental verification of its value.

Marx's research had been motivated by the militant preoccupation of changing the world. Once the theoretical bases of Marx's doctrine were secure, it led him to devote his most serious attention to the study of the objective laws of social development, the condition for the effectiveness of action. As Marx emphasized, 'Men make their own history, but they do not make it just as they please . . . under circumstances chosen by themselves. . . .'[4]

Superficial disciples or excessively hasty or ill-intentioned opponents have frequently mistaken the true originality of Marx's materialism. Opponents likened it more or less to metaphysical materialism and defined it,

---

[3] *Capital*, Modern Library Giant edition, p. 198.
[4] 'The Eighteenth Brumaire of Louis Bonaparte,' *Karl Marx: Selected Works*, vol. II., London, 1943, p. 315.

according to a formula as widely circulated as it was inaccurate, as a reduction of the superior to the inferior. Superficial disciples reduced Marxism to a feeble brand of scientism which reduced philosophy to an extrapolation of the results of science, even to the extent, for example, of understanding 'scientific' history to mean a history in which the future has already been written.

This is a distortion of the very spirit of Marxism which is essentially *a methodology of historical initiative.*

Militant Marxists, whose action would have neither meaning nor foundation if the coming of socialism were guaranteed by an extrinisic necessity, have had to combat these ever-recurring distortions. At the beginning of this century Lenin combatted the 'economism' which yielded to the 'spontaneity' of the movement and put its faith in the automatic integration of socialism into capitalism. This tendency has, ever since, been characteristic of the opportunistic trends which have underestimated the importance of conscience in revolutionary activity.

Still closer to us, the struggle against fatalistic dogmatism was a constant in the work of Maurice Thorez. In 1934, he wrote: 'The breakdown of capitalism is not inevitable.' In 1950, he wrote: 'War is not inevitable.' In 1956: 'Misery is not inevitable.' And, in his studies on pauperization, he rose up 'against the notion of an iron law, a fatalism which hangs over the working class.'

Marxist humanism insists with a special vigour on the specific character which human activity possesses of creating projects, positing ends. It does not look on such activity as the simple resultant or product of the conditions which attended its birth. The emergence of the new —without which there would be no history at all, properly speaking—implies that activity is something other

64

than and more than the sum total of its conditions.

It was in just this sense that Engels insisted on 'the relative independence of superstructures' which, once brought forth by the base, are endowed with 'a movement of their own'. And it was in this sense that Marx, in contrast to any simplist materialism, emphasized that ideas become a material force once they have laid hold of the masses.

For a Marxist, to exist is to create. In distinction to the eighteenth century humanism which was based on a metaphysical conception of 'the essence of man', a Marxist sees existence as preceding essence. Is this to say that it is the same as existentialism? By no means: primarily because freedom possesses an historical character, and then because subjectivity, for a Marxist, is not ignorant of what determines it.

The moment of creation and, along with it, the moments of subjectivity and transcendence, the superseding of the given, are therefore essential in Marxism. If superficial or ill-disposed interpreters of Marx have not always given them their due, the reason is that such interpreters have not seen that Marx, who was aware of the conditions which bestow the greatest effectiveness on this subjectivity and freedom, had to give particular attention to those necessities of which one must be aware before he can free himself from them.

Against the romantics of the revolution or the 'idealists' of the counter-revolution, this is what had to be established first. 'Marx and I,' Engels wrote, are ourselves partly to blame for the fact that younger writers sometimes lay more stress on the economic side than is due to it. We had to emphasize this main principle in opposition to our adversaries, who denied it, and we had not always the time, the place or the opportunity to

E   65

allow the other elements involved in the interaction to come into their rights.'[5]

Only after the phantom of mechanistic materialism has been exorcized can we isolate the originality of the Marxist criticism of religion and the meaning of Marxist atheism.

For earlier materialism, whether that of Epicurus, the eighteenth-century French materialists, or Feuerbach, none of whom isolated, as Marx expressed it, 'the active side of knowledge', and all of whom put into metaphysical opposition a ready-made 'nature', established once for all, and a truth, which is its passive relief, religion, as a deformed, phantasmagorical reflection, could have no reality, no human basis. Religion, for them, was an error pure and simple, a tale made from the whole cloth by 'tyrants and priests', as the eighteenth-century phrase had it.

For Marx, man begins with work. This specifically human activity is characterized by the fact that consciousness anticipates reality: starting off from the conditions of its birth, and in terms of them, it puts forth its own ends, its own projects. Like every ideology, religion is a project, it is a way of breaking away from, transcending the given, of anticipating the real, whether by justifying the existing order or by protesting against it and attempting to transform it.

This first human project assumes the form of myth. Henri Wallon has shown how myth was the detour through the social, preceding the birth of the concept in acting upon the real as well as considering it. 'Among

---

[5] 'Letter 213,' Engels to J. Bloch, September 21, 1890, *Selected Correspondence 1846-1895, Karl Marx and Friedrich Engels,* New York, 1942 ('Marxist Library,' volume 29).

primitive peoples,' Wallon writes, 'the attempt to explain the visible by means of the invisible is not some sort of aberration which turns them away from the real. . . . It is the indispensable condition for every intellectual effort whose purpose is to go beyond the data of ordinary experience. . . .'

Between myth and science, there is, then, a similarity of function. Both provide access to the world of causes through the world of sensible effects. Ritual is a first technology just as a myth is a first science: 'From the time when man's activity was guided by something other than the automatisms which served his needs,' writes Wallon, '. . . from the time when man's activity became subject to the distinctive ritual of the thing itself, when it sought to produce images which surpassed sensible appearances, the great speculative adventure began.'

Ritual and myth release thought from brute perception by distinguishing that which is from that which causes to be and that on which one must act in order to control things.

Thought, mythic and ritualistic at first, will become technology and science, but the goal will always be reproduction, realization, creation.

For a Marxist, therefore, the over-simple, polarized opposition between religion and science which characterized pre-Marxist materialism is not possible. Between religion and science, breach, contradiction and continuity exist simultaneously.

Breach and contradiction exist because the answers given by the religions to the *questions* asked by men, simply from the fact that they are given definitively, as dogmas, bear the mark of myth, that is to say, of a knowledge which poses as timeless while remaining bound up with historical and social conditions.

Religion is, therefore, a human project, but a human project with the air of the mystical about it.

Religion is a human project in the sense that it offers, beyond what is actually given, an *answer* to *questions* asked by man, and calls for practice in conformity with certain demands.

It has the air of the mystical about it, the air, that is to say, of a project which does not take into account the material (historical and social) conditions of its birth, and which, unlike the scientific hypothesis, does not submit to the criterion of practice.

Kant had noted this difference between the two uses of reason: the good use, which submits to experimental verification, and the bad use, which pretends to bypass experience and to develop independently of it.

Marx and, later, Lenin, while analyzing the gnoseological roots of idealism, analyzed the gnoseological roots of religion. As soon as detachment from the immediate, and abstraction too, had become possible, it also became possible to entertain the illusion of the independence of the spiritual from the material, something which is indicated by the first forms of worship of the dead.

The province of science, all along the way, is to reestablish the dialectical tension between abstraction and the subject of the abstraction, and to submit the value of the abstraction to the criterion of practice.

This is the reason why science, despite interdicts and anathemas, has moved continually forward while opposing religion and even forcing it, step by step, to withdraw from one science after another. The process has reached the point where believers who are intimately involved in scientific activity see the vanity of the mythical explanation as soon as the scientific explanation has become possible; they see also the impossibility of situating faith within the temporary imperfections of our knowledge.

Still in all, the notion of project preserves *continuity* between myth and science. At one and the same time, myth is science's past tense and opposite number, which is progressively conquered by science.

Three major events of our era have led the Marxists to systematic reflection on the foundations of their doctrine:

—the amazingly rapid development of science and technology,

—the building of socialism in one-third of the globe,

—the growth of national liberation movements in Asia, Africa and Latin America.

These three converging series of historical events have guided reflection on the basic postulates in the same direction.

a) *The development of science and technology,* as far as the theory of knowledge is concerned, leads to the general substitution of dialectic for intuition and also to the reconstruction of the entire theory of knowledge on the basis of the notion of 'model'.

Contemporary epistemology, Gaston Bachelard's in particular, has uncovered the 'non-Cartesian' character of the development of knowledge. Science does not advance, in linear fashion, from unchangeable data through univocal deductions towards definite and single conclusions. From corrected hypothesis to correctible hypothesis, it proceeds to an unending evolution of global reorganization, according to an interminable dialectic.

The notion of model, as understood in cybernetics, today allows us to take account of the antagonism as well as the unity between myth and scientific hypothesis.

Between the creation of a myth and the construction of a 'model', there is little to be distinguished when seen in terms of the forward movement of the imagination by way of analogy and symbol. And yet there is contrariety as well, since the one demands recourse to practical verification and experimental methods while the other rules them out. Myth is a model which is not verified by experimental method.

The entire theory of knowledge can be thought of today as starting from the notion of 'model'.

This notion permits the Marxist to pass beyond the polarization of knowledge as reflection and knowledge as project. Knowledge is both *reflection* and *project*.

When Marxists speak of 'reflection', they in no way intend thereby to define the laws of knowledge but simply to define its nature, for in only one sense is the analogy of mirror valid: there is no reflection without a reflected object, while it is perfectly possible for an object to exist without a mirror to reflect it. The movement of knowledge, however, cannot be expressed in terms of reflection but in terms of project.

The notion of 'model' has the merit of uniting the two stages of reflection and project.

'Model' indeed implies a reference to an exterior reality, and thereby disposes of the idealist illusion, which Marx denounced in his 'Contribution to the Critique of Political Economy', and which tends to confuse the conceptual 'reproduction' of the real with its 'production'. If one thinks of knowledge as the construction of 'models', *the reflection does not start from knowledge* but actively and progressively constitutes an analogical reproduction which becomes more and more complex, and more and more a likeness.

The 'model' is a reconstruction of the real according to

a human plan. It makes evident 'the active side' of knowledge, the project's role in it.

From Ptolemy's 'model' to Newton's, and then to Einstein's, the structure and the laws of development of the universe are presented in progressively less mythical fashion, even though myth is never totally eliminated or science totally lacking.

The conception of 'model' permits Marxism to think clearly about the dialectic of relative truth and absolute truth, suggested by Lenin in *Materialism and Empirio-Criticism,* by showing the internal relationships of continuity and breach between myth and science, ideological illusion and scientific theory, and the experienced and the objective.

b) *The building of socialism* has presented analogous problems. To begin with, after the far-reaching criticism which was demanded by the revelations at the Twentieth Congress of the Communist Party of the Soviet Union, it made evident the fact that a *plurality of models of socialism* was both possible and necessary. At the present time, the working relationship between central planning and initiative from below is the central problem which faces the building of socialism.

In any event, it is now out of the question to think of the building of socialism in the ingenuous terms of syllogism and idyll: the road that must be followed is a road of agony which lies between the dramatic epic of five-year plans and the tragedies of self-management.

The accent has now been placed on *the problems of subjectivity.* This development has occurred because of the inescapable abandonment of old values and the birth-pangs which accompany the creation of new ones. A similar development has occurred at every turning point in history. After the tremendous social and spiritual upheavals of the French Revolution, which threw doubt on all traditional values, Kierkegaard's existentialism appeared on the scene to contend with the majestic system of Hegel. Similarly, after the social and moral renewal which accompanied the October Socialist Revolution, the greatest spiritual event of our century, a quarter of a century of intellectual hardening of the arteries within Marxism has been followed by the vigorous reappearance of the problems of subjectivity, choice and spiritual responsibility. The existentialism of Heidegger and Sartre has thrown a veil over eventual solution, but it has nevertheless emphasized the seriousness and depth of the questions presented. To the extent that Marxism has failed to answer these questions adequately, youth has turned elsewhere to seek the answer which it is our job today to seek, though we may not yet fully discover.

c) *The growth of national liberation movements* in Asia, Africa and Latin America has aggravated these problems.

During the last few years, our horizon has been suddenly enlarged. A qualitative change in the rhythm of historical development has occurred, and not simply because of scientific and technological discoveries but also because of another fact of immense significance: decolonization.

The West—Europe and North America—is no longer the sole centre of historical initiative or the sole creator of values.

Though the peoples of Asia, the Arab world and the countries of black Africa have not produced a technology as effective as our own, it would still be fatal for contemporary humanism if we were to neglect to seek and to acknowledge the values created by peoples whose original

72

development was arrested by colonization and whose own history was taken away from them.

Marxism, whose ambition is to inherit all prior culture, could not possibly reduce this culture to the strictly Western traditions of classical German philosophy, English economy, French socialism, Greek rationalism, and the technicism which grew out of the Renaissance.

It is part of Marxism's universal vocation to put forth its roots in the culture of all peoples.

There is no question of denying or abandoning rationalistic and technological tradition for the sake of the irrational, but only of integrating all the forces inherent in life within a rationalism which is enriched by such contributions.

Neither is there any question of going beyond science, but only of reflecting upon the variant forms of humanity represented by the non-Western civilizations and the different models they provide of the basic relationship with being. These civilizations and cultures force us to reflect on our own basic positions, to become aware of their contingent character, to conceive of other possible relationships, to see our own choices in some kind of perspective. This is a major contribution to our effort to effect a return to what is basic.

With this as a point of departure, the Marxists have been able to rethink and to relive their theory of religion.

It is, of course, true that in France, from 1937 on, Maurice Thorez had called for a new attitude towards Christians. But what has, since then, been called the initiative of 'the outstretched hand' to believers—and has remained a constant in French Communist Party policy—has frequently been given a narrow and restrictive interpretation that might be summed up in the formula: 'We hold out our hand to Catholic workers as *workers* and not as *Catholics.*' Such a formula betrays a rather mechanical view of the relationship of base with superstructure and either denies or underestimates the relative independence of superstructures and their consequent action on the base.

To proceed in this fashion is to misconstrue the possibility and reality of the positive contributions of Christianity, as Christianity, to the development of universal culture and even to the revolutionary movement of the oppressed masses. And yet Maurice Thorez was unquestionably aware of this dual aspect from 1937 on.

Thorez wrote: 'The promise of a redeemer brightens the first page of human history, the Catholic says; the promise of a universal city, reconciled in labour and in love, sustains the efforts of the proletariat as it strives towards the happiness of all men. . . .'

And he added:

'Christianity's progressive role appears in the effort to realize charity and solidarity, in the attempt to bring about fairer and more peaceable relationships among men during the feudal era, in the concern of religious communities—communist groupings in intention, in fact, and in action—which assumed the mission of preserving, developing and transmitting to future ages the sum total of human knowledge and the artistic treasures of the past. Who can think without emotion of the centuries which saw the towers of our cathedrals rising towards the sky, those gems of popular art whose every stone, alive for all who can understand, cries out against the fable of cheerless middle ages?

'I often draw the comparison between the builders of cathedrals, alive with the ardent faith "which moves mountains" and makes great achievements possible, and the builders of the new city of socialism . . . who cause to rise up from the ground . . . those magnificent monuments which today proclaim the vibrant drive of Communism.'

But, in every period of class-domination, this exalted ideal of love has been used by the ruling class and by its clergy as a heavenly recompense for earth's miseries and servitudes. The promise of unity 'in Christ' was used as an alibi to disarm the rebellion of the humiliated and offended. But to condemn the slave's revolt, in the name of love, is to be an accomplice in the master's oppression.

It is Communism alone, as Gorki wrote, which will create the true conditions of a society in which love will cease to be a promise, or a moral law, and will become the objective law of the entire society.

If we are Communists, it is precisely because we are struggling for this classless society.

This is why we perfectly understand the need, brought forth by suffering, for perfect communion and for a love so all-embracing that those who suffered never believed they could find it anywhere but in God. Indeed, we find it a beautiful thing that man, in his suffering, conceived such dreams, such hopes, conceived the infinite love of Christ. It is this act of faith that proves that man never considers himself wholly defeated. And thus he witnesses to his greatness. This is why we neither despise nor criticize the Christian for his faith, his love, his dreams, his hopes. Our own task is to labour and to struggle, lest they remain eternally distant or illusory. Our task as Communists is to draw near to man in his most glorious dreams and his most sublime hopes, to draw near to him in a real and practical way, so that Christians themselves might find here on our earth a beginning of their heaven.

These are the bases for a common struggle by Communists and Catholics, for a noble rivalry between them in the human contest.

A Catholic recently put it thus: 'I say that, whatever happens, the man who is free and who freely chooses, without being stupefied by existence, will never be separated from God. And you say that when man is no longer in need of distraction from his misery, when he no longer feels the need to escape from awful necessity by telling stories to himself, such a free and independent man will do without God. . . . The issue thus joined, I am ready to argue.' A fine challenge, and one which must be accepted.

When a Christian says to us: 'Capitalism, with its crises, its wars, the threats by which it burdens the country's freedoms, capitalism is an inhuman regime and the enemy of the human person,' our answer is: Now we have a solid basis for agreement within the religious or philosophical perspective of each of us.

This conception was espoused and brilliantly developed by Louis Aragon during the Resistance not only in poems like 'La rose et le réséda,' which exalted the common sacrifice of 'the one who believed in heaven' and 'the one who did not', but also in essays such as 'De l'exactitude historique en poésie'. In the latter, while emphasizing, in a fine outburst of patriotism, what Marx termed the movement of 'protest' of religious faith, he wrote these self-critical lines: 'An old-fashioned materialist like me had been condemning the Christian extraordinary as opposed to freedom's different extraordinaries. . . . The relationship which derives from the negation of the real by the extraordinary is essentially ethical in nature, and the extraordinary is always the materialization of a moral symbol which is in violent opposition to the morality of the world in which it springs up. . . .

I hope that my companions in arms and in sworn allegiance who bear within their hearts a large cross will not be vexed to learn I am not ashamed to say that I now respect, that I have learned to respect their faith which I shall never share. How much that is generous, that is human, in this divine faith. How much that, when confronted by my nation's enemy, sang in harmony with my unbelief—a conception of man which is possible for Communist and Christian, but for a Nazi, never. . . . And this, I am certain, does not make of me a more mediocre materialist than I was in 1930.' More than twenty years later, when in *Le Fou d'Elsa* Aragon devotes one of his most beautiful poems to St John of the Cross, he reminds us of the major truth that Marxism would be the poorer if St Paul and St Augustine, St Teresa of Avila, Pascal and Claudel, the Christian meaning of transcendence of love were to become foreign to it.

In reflecting on what Marx called 'the human depth' of Christianity, we have had a chance to suggest what Marxists must assimilate from the rich Christian heritage. Marxist humanism, when it takes its position, as Marx insisted it must, on the other side of what is merely negative in atheism, has an interest in the questions men ask about the meaning of their life and their death, about the problem of their origin and their end, about the demands of their thought and their heart.

If the greatness of religion is proven by the exigency of answering these questions, its weakness and its defectiveness lie in pretending to give them a dogmatic answer, which must ever be bound up with a certain stage of knowledge, and which, while bearing the stigma of the transitory inadequacies of the age, is offered as definitive, and even as sacred.

Marxist criticism rejects illusory answers, but it does

not reject the authentic aspiration which aroused them. Beyond the myths about the origin, end and meaning of life, beyond the alienated notions of transcendence and death, there exists the concrete dialectic of finite and infinite, and this remains a living reality as long as we remain aware *that it is not in the order of answer but in the order of question.*

Consequently, religion cannot be considered solely in terms of alienation: *alienation is in the answers, but not in the questions.*

What is true of knowledge is also true of action: man achieves a growing mastery over nature, society and his own future, but if his power ceases to grow, he will be ever-militant and never-triumphant, if only because he comes up against the final limitation, which is death. He no more arrives at the total 'beatitude' to which he aspires than he arrives at 'total knowledge'. Once again, religion claims to provide a metaphysical answer to this exigency. 'Religion', writes Marx in 'The Jewish Question', 'is simply the recognition of man in a roundabout fashion; that is, through an intermediary'.[6]

On the level of knowledge, the religions, starting from a real need, transformed into answer something which pertained to the order of question. In precisely the same fashion, on the level of action, the religions, and Christianity above all, transformed an exigency into a promise —and even into a presence: from the exigency of mediation, they passed over to the presence of a mediator.

Once again, *alienation is in the promise and in the affirmation of presence, but not in the exigency which aroused it and which Marxism must take command of* by finding again, underneath the myth, the aspiration which brought it forth.

[6] *Karl Marx: Early Writings*, p. 11.

Realization of What is Basic by Marxists

This offers some response to Father Metz's first question. Yes, the fully developed man in Communism's classless society will be more of a questioner because he will be more fully a man. Yes, the future will be filled with questions which surpass and transcend anything we can imagine about the future. Yes, man will always be capable of an always greater future. For us, Communism is not the end of history, but the end of prehistory, man's prehistory which is made up of the jungle-like encounters common to all class societies. 'This social formation,' Marx writes in his 'Contribution to the Critique of Political Economy,' 'constitutes . . . the closing chapter of the prehistoric stage of human society.'[7]

Authentically human history will begin with Communism. It will be a history which is no longer made up of class struggle and war. Engels writes, in his 'Ludwig Feuerbach and the Outcome of Classical German Philosophy'. 'Just as knowledge is unable to reach a perfected termination in a perfect, ideal condition of humanity, so is history unable to do so.'[8] Contradictions will not be abolished, but they will no longer be bloody contradictions among human beings. Then, starting with questions which will no longer seek in alienated answers a coward's repose, the endless dialectic of freedom made one with creation will flower.

Past the violent dialectic which provides the impetus for our prehistory, there will spread forth the constructive dialectic of the struggle of men united in conquering nature, and the dialectic of dialogue first envisioned by Socrates.

When I wrote *Karl Marx*, I offered an answer to this

[7] *Selected Works I*, London, 1947, p. 301.
[8] See Translation, *ibid.*, p. 359.

question. 'This creation will have the marks of an aesthetic creation. By this I mean, first of all, that it will be a creation which is not demanded by any need other than the specifically human need to create and to create oneself. . . . Why should man be unable to create except when goaded on by need and anxiety, particularly when the Christians themselves have conceived of a God whose creation was not a necessary emanation, but a free gift of love?'

And thus we answer the remaining two questions of Father Metz and Père Cottier. Whence does Marxism derive its negative capability except from a presence which lies 'behind the question'?

Marxism asks the same questions as the Christian does, is influenced by the same exigency, lives under the same tension towards the future. The crucial factor is that Marxism does not consider itself entitled—because it is a critical rather than a dogmatic philosophy—to transform its question into answer, its exigency into presence. 'O ever-active Spirit, how I feel your presence!' wrote Goethe. Marxism, by reason of its Faustian and Fichtean inspiration, does not succumb to the temptation to affirm, behind the activity, a being who is its source. My thirst does not prove the existence of the spring. For the Marxist, the infinite is absence and exigency, while for the Christian, it is promise and presence.

There is thus indicated an indisputable divergence between the Promethean conception of freedom as creation, and the Christian conception of freedom as grace and assent.

For a Christian, transcendence is the act of God who comes towards him and summons him. For a Marxist, it is a dimension of man's activity which goes out beyond itself towards its far-off being.

This far-off being, on the horizon of all our projects, is, in Father Rahner's terms, absolute future. Only for us it is a human future, and as such it is not a set future, which would of necessity be limited by the alienation of our present projects, which are always those (as Father Metz rightly emphasizes) of an alienated man in an alienated society—but a future always moving and expanding, a future which grows in direct proportion to our progress. Alienation in such circumstances would consist in the arresting of our project at one stage in the endless realization of man. This is why the project of revolution is the contrary of the utopia which consists precisely in the naïve and enclosed project of the man who joins to alienation the ignorance of alienation and the ingenuous illusion of transcending it.

Father Girardi asserted, in his address at Salzburg: 'M. Garaudy asks us if Christians think that Marxism impoverishes man?' We answer him frankly: 'In the measure that Marxism believes that the earth can be enough for him, yes, it impoverishes him.'

Marxists are so little content with the earth that they assume the primary task of transforming it. This is not a play on words or an evasion intended to dodge the heavenly dimension of man's destiny. For the transformation of the earth, as we see it, is not solely its social and technical reorganization, and the institution of new economic and political relationships among men; it is also a profound spiritual metamorphosis of man. To liberate man from all alienation, material and moral, is to accomplish, within the continuing creation of man by man, a new and decisive step towards increased hominisation, a step as important as the invention of the tool, through which the human branch broke away from the common trunk of animality by conquering consciousness.

This new frontier of hominization, making of every man a man, questioning and creative, will mark a new detachment from the earth. The detachment, this time, will be from all the alienations which have been crystallized for thousands of years and have become so thoroughly customary as to seem to us like a *given* nature, like earth itself. It will free the spiritual energies of each man and of all men with such force that it is absolutely impossible—for us who are caught in the alienations of our prehistory—to imagine their nature and their use. This future, open on the infinite, is the only transcendence which is known to us as atheists.

Our answer to Father Girardi is made in a fraternal manner: What makes us atheists is not our sufficiency, our satisfaction with ourselves and with the earth, with some sort of limitation on our project. The reason is that we, from our experience, similar to the Christian's, of the inadequacy of all relative and partial being, do not conclude to a presence, that of the 'one necessary', which answers to our anguish and impatience.

If we reject the very name of God, it is because the name implies a presence, a reality, whereas it is only an exigency which we live, a never-satisfied exigency of totality and absoluteness, of omnipotence as to nature and of perfect loving reciprocity of consciousness.

We can live this exigency, and we can act it out, but we cannot conceive it, name it or expect it. Even less can we hypostasize it under the name of transcendence. Regarding this totality, this absolute, I can say everything except: It is. For what it is is always deferred, and always growing, like man himself.

If we want to give it a name, the name will not be that of God, for it is impossible to conceive of a God who is always in process of making himself, in process of being born. The most beautiful and the most exalted name which can be given to this exigency is the name of man. To refuse it to him is to strip him of one of his dimensions, and his essential, specific dimension, for man is precisely he who is not. This exigency in man is, I think, the flesh of your God.

We are undoubtedly living, Christians and Marxists alike, the exigency of the same infinite, but yours is presence while ours is absence.

Is it to impoverish man, to tell him that he lives as an incomplete being, that everything depends upon him, that the whole of our history and its significance is played out within man's intelligence, heart and will, and nowhere else, that we bear full responsibility for this; that we must assume the risk, every step of the way, since, for us atheists, nothing is promised and no one is waiting?

Do not call pride something which is not our choice but the simple awareness of our condition and the humble admission that we cannot say: I know. We are incapable of saying that God, as the absolute future of man, is already present, and that we move already within him.

I think that Marxist atheism deprives man only of the illusion of certainty, and that the Marxist dialectic, when lived in its fullness, is ultimately richer in the infinite and more demanding still than the Christian transcendence.

To be sure, it is undoubtedly such only because it bears within itself the extraordinary Christian heritage, which it must investigate still more. Living Marxism, which has proven its fruitfulness and its effectiveness in history, in political economy, in revolutionary struggle and in the building of socialism, owes it to itself in philosophy to work out a more profound theory of subjectivity, one

83

which is not subjectivist, and a more profound theory of transcendence, one which is not alienated.

In this investigation we can learn a great deal from Christianity, and it would be one of the tragedies of history—and so much lost time for humanity—if the dialogue between Christians and Marxists and their co-operation for mutual enrichment and for the common building of the future, the city of men, the total man, were still longer to be spoiled, perhaps even prevented, by the weight of the past.

The conflict between us is of a thousand years' duration.

We shall not be able to dispose of it unless we face it frankly.

A balance sheet of grievances was drawn up in Marx's lapidary phrase of 1843: 'Religion is the opium of the people.'

It is well worth asking the question whether it is true, judging from a purely historical and sociological point of view, that religion has been and is an opium of the people.

It seems impossible not to answer in the affirmative.

Since Constantine, the teaching of the Church, in its official form and during the major part of its history, has curbed or combatted the struggles of the oppressed by locating in another world the conquest of justice, freedom and happiness, by bestowing a legitimacy as of divine right on the established order, and by teaching resignation in the face of exploitation and oppression.

If we look to the experience of the West, we see that the masters of Christian thought have made all class domination legitimate: slavery, serfdom, the salary system.

Realization of What is Basic by Marxists

St Augustine writes in *The City of God* (Book XIX, Chapter 15): 'Slavery is a punishment for sin. . . . And this is why the Apostle (*Eph.* 4. 5) admonishes slaves to be subject to their masters, and to serve them with good heart and good will, so that, if they cannot be freed from servitude, they might find freedom in servitude, by serving not in fear but in love, until the time when iniquity passes away and every human mastery is brought to nothing and God will be all in all.'

The noble ambition of Spartacus has ceased to be.

The theme developed by St Augustine in regard to slavery will be taken up again by St Thomas Aquinas in the age of serfdom: 'Slavery among men is natural. . . . The slave, in regard to his master, is an instrument. . . . Between a master and his slave there is a special right of domination' (*Summa Theologiae*, IIa-IIae, q. 57, aa 3 & 4). This right even implies the right of the master to beat his slave (*ibid.* q. 65, a 2).

Bossuet will repeat the same argument, centuries later, to justify the treatment of Negroes, in his *Cinquième avertissement à Jurieu.*

The basic thesis will be developed in all its generality by Pope Pius X on December 18, 1903: 'Human society as established by God is made up of unequal elements. . . . Accordingly, it is in conformity with the order of human society as established by God that there be rulers and ruled, employers and employees, learned and ignorant, nobles and plebeians.'[9]

There evidently flows from this thesis a social doctrine based on resignation. The encyclical *Quadragesimo anno* (1931) explicitly drew this conclusion: 'The workers will

---

[9] *Fin Dalla Prima*, December 18, 1903, *Motu proprio* on popular Christian action.

accept without rancour the place which Divine Providence has assigned to them.'

From the political point of view, and looking to recent French history for support, we see that the official Church has not terminated its alliance with the ruling power and with all backward-looking forces, from the theory of the 'divine right' to that of the 'Holy Alliance', from the *Terreur blanche* of 1815 to the Falloux Law following the revolt of June 1848, from the consecration of Paris to the Sacred Heart, in expiation for the Commune, to the Dreyfus Affair and the support of the regime of Marshal Pétain.

As Father José Gomez Caffarena wrote in *Razón y Fé*, in December, 1964: 'By a sad paradox, Christianity, the religion of love, has historically served to cover over the worst of egotisms.'

The fact is one which must be recalled, not for the morose pleasure of exhuming the past, but to avoid idealizing the dialogue. For what makes recognizing the Christian contribution to the conception of man and the realization of the total man a matter of difficulty and doubt for many unbelievers is precisely the undeniable historical support which has frequently been given, and is given still, by the churches to the forces which oppress and exploit men.

Taking this tragic difficulty into account, the editors of *Abside*, the review of the Jesuit Novitiate of the Theological Faculty of Burgos, wrote in September, 1964: 'Neither our morality, nor our Church, nor our God are those of the workers because they are those of the owners.'

Is this tantamount to saying that religion is the opium of the people? With like forcefulness, we answer: No. The Marxist conception of religion cannot be reduced and is not reduced to this simple formula.

86

Realization of What is Basic by Marxists

As the Spanish Communist leader Santiago Alvarez puts it in the *Nouvelle Revue Internationale*, the theoretical monthly of the Communist and Labour parties, for June, 1965: 'As used by the exploiting and ruling classes, religion has been and remains an opium. But this is merely one aspect of Marx's thought. If we stopped at it, we would find it impossible to seek and to discover a solution to the theoretical and social problems which social reality presents, problems which are presented to us in our relationship with believers today.'

The thesis that religion always and everywhere turns man away from action, from struggle, and from work is in flagrant contradiction to the facts of history.

What is more, this was never Marx's thesis.

In the very text in which we find the famous formula, 'Religion is the opium of the people', Marx emphasizes, several lines further on, that *'religious* suffering is at the same time an *expression* of real suffering and a *protest* against real suffering'.[10] We have here an initial dialectical approach to the religious fact.

This dialectical conception alone permits an understanding of the history of Christianity by distinguishing, at each stage along the way, the reflection and the protest, the opium and the leaven, the faith and the ideology, the Constantinian and the apocalyptic, the existential exigency and the alienation from it.

The basic Christian message constituted a radical break from Greek humanism by introducing a new attitude towards the world of nature and of human relationships: a free relationship between the acting subject and the cosmos; but the truth is that the message was soon clothed

[10] 'Contribution to the Critique of Hegel's Philosophy of Right,' *Karl Marx: Early Writings,* p. 43.

87

in a syncretistic ideology which masked it and submerged it under the mainstreams of the hellenistic world, notably:

—*Stoicism,* the art of living in times of stress, which taught progressive independence from the vicissitudes of the world by leaving it so as the better to contemplate it.

—*the astral religions,* which were a reflection of the feeling that men had been handed over to a destiny which was both chance and inescapable necessity, within a world which had ceased to be a homeland,

—*the mystery religions,* which were based on the conviction that man did not become master of his destiny by the power of his mind and acts, and also on the quest for superhuman forces which could come to man's aid and save him. The central figure of these religions of salvation and redemption was a young god who dies and who then triumphs over death by resurrection, such as Attis, Adonis or Mithras,

Gnosis, the myth about the destiny of the soul, born in light, fallen in the shadows of earthly existence and the prison of the body, and whose deliverance requires an ascension and a return to the light.

These various metaphysics of a world in an impasse such as confronted the Roman Empire in the first century of our era are conveyed by Christianity even though they are not what is essential in Christianity.

This is something which it is important to emphasize. If we have attributed so much importance to the research of theologians, Protestants like Bultmann or Catholics like Father Rahner, which has led towards isolating what is basic and specifically Christian in Christianity, the reason is that the bulk of the criticism has been directed, on the one hand, against the *Constantinian traditions* of the Church, that is, to its historical alliance with the classes and powers of oppression, and, on the other hand, against the Hellenistic and Roman *ideology* in which the original faith is caught.

Engels, in his studies on primitive Christianity, made no mistake. Gilbert Mury, in a study on *Le christianisme primitif et le monde moderne*, has excellently emphasized what Engels had neatly distinguished as the 'religious need' (faith) and the 'school philosophy' (ideology) in his 1882 article on 'Bruno Bauer and Primitive Christianity'. Engels, analyzing primitive Christianity through the text of the Book of Revelation, shows how it was founded on the base of a universal protest—however impotent— against generalized exploitation and oppression. Engels sees as a 'revolutionary element' 'the faith of these first pugnacious communities [which] is utterly different from that of the later triumphant Church. . . . Everything which comes later is a Western, Greco-Roman addition.' This distinction recurs several times during the course of his argument. After describing the primitive faith of apocalyptic Christianity as 'forced and confused need', he adds: 'The definitive elaboration of dogmas and morality is the work of a later period.' Lenin makes the same distinction when he speaks, in 'State and Revolution', of the Christians of the fourth century who forget 'when their worship has become the State Religion, the democratic revolutionary spirit of primitive Christianity'.[11]

Later biblical and New Testament research, notably the studies based on the discovery of the Dead Sea Scrolls, beginning in 1947, have, despite a number of uncertainties about chronology, made possible a still better discerning of the basic nucleus which antedated the syncretistic ideologies, and a still better tracing of the

[11] *Collected Works of V. I. Lenin*, vol. 21, New York, 1932, p. 184.

filtration between primordial Christian preaching and Old Testament Jewish prophetism, which held that God was not to be discovered in present reality (whether in nature or in history) but in the future. God is the God who is always coming. God's transcendence is not conceived, as in the dualism of the Greeks, as a form imposed on matter, but as a permanent future, an appeal, an exigency. Christ, in a sense, prolongs the eschatological message of the Old Testament prophets and the Judaism of the dispersion of Israel. Once Israel had ceased to be a nation, God no longer revealed himself in the history of the nation but acquired a universal meaning. Jesus, continuing the prophets' protest against Jewish legalism, goes much further still: he announces that the times have been accomplished and that the present is the time for decision. Henceforth, to believe will mean being wholly open to the future. Man is no longer conceived as a fragment of the city and then of the cosmic whole. No longer is he defined as *logos* but as power of choice, as responsible will to respond or not to respond to the call of God by breaking away from his past. Obedience to God, in this new voluntary covenant of the Christian, is verified concretely in the presence of the neighbour, by the militant love one has for him.

This primitive Christian message, a radical departure from the Greco-Latin conception of the world and of man, soon finds expression, in the next generation, that of the redaction of the Gospels, in the language of the cosmology, myths and philosophy of the Greeks of the hellenistic period. So true is this that a superficial observer could easily think that he sees in Christianity just another variant of neo-Platonism or Gnostic myth. What is more, an entire Christian tradition can root us in this error.

However, even in a deceptive language which translates into physical terms the spiritual experience of radical freedom, the originality of the Christian contribution is apparent when compared with the aesthetic and rational humanism of the Greeks. At the beginning of the fourth century, Lactantius made a striking contrast between the two attitudes towards man and the world. 'What the Stoics argue is in favour of the divinity of the celestial beings actually proves the contrary; for if they think that the celestial beings are gods because of their regular and rational course, they are mistaken indeed. . . . Precisely because the celestial beings cannot depart from their pre-scribed orbits, it is apparent that they are not gods. If they were gods, they would be seen to be borne here and there just like living beings on the earth, who go where they wish because their wills are free.'[12]

Here again, a superficial reading would lead us to retain only the disclaimer of the rational, since the naïve transcription into physical terms leads to a confusion of the affirmation of the subjective moment, by which man inserts his own initiative into the world, with a breach in physical causality and the order of nature.

We can here grasp, almost at its source, the fatal mis-understanding, always being born anew in Christian thought, which permits the confusion of the irrational with the act through which human initiative and prac-tice bring forth a new rationality from the very heart of living reason.

The precise meaning of openness to the future has thus degenerated, in popular apologetics, into an attempt to slip faith in between the temporary defects of knowledge and to lower the idea of God to the point of making it,

[12] *The Divine Institutes*, Book II, Chapter 5.

in Père Dubarle's phrase, 'the petty supplement to our intellectual inadequacies'.

It was this that Père Teilhard so violently reacted against. 'The classical apologists,' he writes in *Le Christianisme et le Monde* (1933), 'found their principal support in miracles, whose appearance, were we to believe them, was the "reagent" proper to "true" religion. Without denying—quite the contrary!—the possibility or even the likelihood, in the area of the "true" religion, of an unexpected loosening up of determinisms, due to some sort of super-animation of nature under the influence of a divine radiance, we must nevertheless recognize that the thought of the miraculous no longer acts effectively on our minds. The establishment of the miraculous creates so many historical or physical problems that there are probably many Christians today who remain believers not *because of* but *despite* the wonders related in Scripture.'

We have here a meaningful example of the effort which is necessary to discern what is basic in the symbols and physical metaphors which were used to express, at archaic stages of culture, the sense of openness on an absolute future, the certainty, proper to faith, of the possibility of liberation from the burdens of the past, and of a new beginning.

Efforts of this kind, which are more and more frequent in our age, help Marxists to see the vanity of the smug illusion—bequeathed to the proletariat by the French eighteenth century which radically mistook the specific quality of the religious fact—that good scientific propaganda will make it possible to do away with religion.

The truth is that the advance of science makes it possible to push back all the superstitious forms of the successive ideologies in which faith has at all times been clothed. This is why theology has continually drawn back before science. When we study, in the majority of religious publications intended for the general public, the gross types of apologetic employed, from the falsification of the meaning of scientific concepts (in a French magazine like *Planète,* for example) to the pure and simple thaumaturgy of a certain 'good Catholic press', we see the absolute necessity for a systematic struggle on the scientific level against this 'religious' propaganda which pretends to teach Christianity with the images of the grossest superstitions. We sometimes get the impression, if we compare the writings of Teilhard, Père Dubarle or Father Rahner with the so-called 'popular' publications, that two different religions are being taught under the same name. When we are given the explanation that the question is simply one of putting this teaching at the disposal of the 'simple', we cannot escape the thought that this kind of attitude implies a deep paternalistic contempt for people whose development they thus undertake to arrest by maintaining them within the limitations of an intellectual world which has long since been left behind.

The struggle against such a degradation of man is one which we can and must lead with those Christians at our side who are most closely connected with the scientific world.

Science is thus of assistance in bringing about the rejection of superstition, magic and myth.

Does it affect what is basic in religion? We do not think that it does.

A resolutely rationalistic and spontaneously materialistic *savant* like the physicist Max Planck entitles the final chapter of his *Scientific Autobiography and Other Papers* 'Religion and Natural Science'. He poses this problem: Does the progress of the natural sciences involve, in the long run or in the short run, the decline of religion?

His first answer is: 'The faith in miracles must yield ground, step by step, before the steady and firm advance of the forces of science, and its total defeat is indubitably a mere matter of time.'[13]

After showing that moral truths (such as the free power of man to intervene in nature, transform it, and thereby even be transformed himself) are expressed, historically, through symbols corresponding to the physical image which has been made of the world in each and every age, Planck stresses the historically relative character of the religious symbol which, with its physical images, 'never represents an absolute value but is always only a more or less imperfect sign of something higher and not directly accessible to human senses'.[14]

'Through . . . attacks against symbols,' writes Planck, '[the atheists] expect to hurt religion itself.'[15] But this is to mistake the specific character of faith and to confuse it with the always transitory ideologies in which it is expressed.

It is proper to add that all the supposedly 'scientific' attempts at Christian apologetics are ascribable to the same failure of appreciation: an astronomer like Canon Lemaître, for example, forcing himself to prop up the most naïve conceptions of creationism with the most sophisticated interpretations of the 'theory of the expanding universe', or a hurried apologist trying to exploit what certain physicists have called 'physical indetermin-

[13] Max Planck, *Scientific Autobiography and Other Papers*, New York, 1949, p. 155.
[14] *ibid.*, p. 163.
[15] *ibid.*, *loc. cit.*

94

ism' as a way of infiltrating human freedom and divine grace into cracks in the rational!

As against such conceptions of God, there is still validity in Laplace's remark that he had no need of this hypothesis to establish his cosmogonic theory, and in Bichat's remark: 'I found no soul at the end of scalpel.' Such 'physical' conceptions of God forced Pasteur to leave his beliefs in the cloak-room when he entered his laboratory. Science plays a beneficial role here (both for itself and for authentic faith) by mercilessly chasing away these images of God tailored, like idols, in matter. Every time theology intrudes into the domain of science, it will inexorably end up defeated. This is not one of the least important aspects of the return to what is basic: faith can only be itself if it completely abandons the ground of science.

Still, the essential debate between Christians and atheists is not on the scientific plane but on the moral plane.

The thing that defines atheism is the reducing of the religious fact to the human fact: it is men who have created gods.

Max Planck thus poses the central question: 'Does that higher power which stands behind the religious symbols and lends them their essential signficance, dwell solely in the human mind?'[16]

It is true that we cannot take a step in the domain of thought or action without affirming, by our act itself, the possibility and necessity of an order. At the root of every scientific hypothesis which seeks to realize a new unification of appearances, there is the postulate of the certain existence, outside of us and independently of us, of a

[16] Planck, *op. cit.*, p. 166.

rational order. My *project* is to reflect it. At the root of every political or moral enterprise which seeks to realize a higher form of unification of the world—such as the classless society of Communism will be—there is the postulate that history has a meaning and that the realization of the total man is a realizable project. The philosophy of the absurd is neither for the learned man nor for the revolutionary.

Neither is it for the believer.

Another physicist, Werner Heisenberg, firmly defining his attitude towards the world in *The Physicist's Conception of Nature*, in the chapter entitled 'Faith in Our Task', writes as follows: 'What is, and always has been, our mainspring, is faith . . . faith in our task in this world. Here, faith obviously does not mean that we hold this or that to be true. If I have faith, it means that I have decided to do something and am willing to stake my life on it. When Columbus started on his first voyage into the west, he believed that the earth was round and small enough to be circumnavigated. He did not think that this was right in theory alone, but he staked his whole existence on it. . . . "I believe so that I may act; I act so that I may understand." This saying is relevant not only to the first voyages round the world, it is relevant to the whole domain of science. . . .'[17]

This faith animates all those, believers or unbelievers, who believe, to use an expression of Teilhard's, that the universe is moving forward and that our task as men is to make it move forward.

A profound divergence nevertheless subsists between Christians and Marxists, and it is important to locate it exactly.

[17] New York, 1958, pp. 65-66.

Faith in our task does not imply for us Marxists any reference to the presence and call of a God. Earlier successes of thought and action in the process of humanizing nature and humanizing history give us, we think, sufficient strength to pursue the human epic begun more than a million years ago. We freely concede that we live out this certainty in risk, for no one and nothing guarantees us victory in advance. But no one and nothing permits us to assert that such a guarantee exists, either.

Faith in God causes in the Christian the assent which we live as creation, although for both this consists in openness to the future and supersedure. The certainties which we postulate at the term of our effort are postulated by the Christian at the source.

But what remains is that we are both experiencing the same tension.

And what matters is that completely human faith in our task does not mutilate man of any of the dimensions which have been won because of faith in God, and that faith in a transcendent God never limits or curbs faith in the human task.

Every other divergence is not a religious divergence.

Polemic on the *institution,* such as that on the social role of the Church or the behaviour of socialist states or Communist parties, is a *political and historical discussion.*

Polemic on religious *ideology* and Marxist theory is a *scientific and philosophical discussion.*

On the level of institution and ideology, two human *projects* meet and are capable of enriching one another; the problem of atheism and faith cannot be the basis either for prejudice or for hindrance.

It is undoubtedly for the Christians to say what Marxism contributes to enable their faith to be incarnate in historical reality and to become an effective force in the struggle to create the political and social conditions of the realization of the total man.

But, as Marxists, we cannot evade the quest for what Marxism itself, as a conception of the world which is the basis for a methodology of historical initiative, owes to Christianity as a religion of the absolute future and as a contributing factor in the exploration of the two essential dimensions of man: subjectivity and transcendence.

We cannot, without impoverishing ourselves, forget Christianity's basic contribution: the change in man's attitude towards the world, preparing a place for the subjectivity which St Augustine, despite his Platonism and its resultant conservatism, so wonderfully began to explore.

The aspect of 'protest', linked to the Christian discovery of the importance of the moment of 'subjectivity', and the 'apocalyptic' pole of Christianity, as opposed to the 'Constantinian' pole, reappear in many historical movements in which religious faith, far from being an opium, plays the role of a leaven in the people's struggle. Marx and Engels showed examples of this in the case of John Hus and Thomas Muenzer. Protest here took on a militant aspect and expanded into insurrection: 'It demanded,' writes Engels in *The Peasant War in Germany*, 'that the conditions of equality in primitive Christianity be . . . recognized as norms for civil society. From the equality of men before God, it made the inference to civil equality and even, in part, to human equality.'[18] Engels recalls the themes of this revolutionary struggle: 'Heaven was to be sought in this life, not beyond, and it was, according to Muenzer, the task of the

[18] Friedrich Engels, *The Peasant War in Germany;* cf. ET, New York, 1926, p. 54.

98

believers to establish Heaven, the kingdom of God, here
on earth.'[19] When the armed uprising broke out in the
autumn of 1513, the banner of the *Bundschuh* insurgents
bore the inscription: 'Lord, sustain your divine Justice.'
Engels concludes: 'There is more than one Communist
sect of modern times which, even on the eve of the March
Revolution (1848), did not possess a theoretical arsenal
as rich as that of the Muenzerian sects of the sixteenth
century.'[20]

The same sort of demonstration is possible in regard to
John Hus, and it is significant that the Catholic Church
today envisages his 'rehabilitation' along with Galileo's.

In an effort to deny, against all the evidence, that religious faith could play a progressive role in given historical
conditions, there is sometimes a certain amount of quib-
bling over Engels' remark that a particular revolutionary
movement assumed 'religious' form, and it is suggested
that 'form' should be interpreted to exclude content and,
especially, any real effectiveness.

The denial that this 'form' is at the same time a *force*
which exercises a reciprocal action on the base which
generated it constitutes a regression to the mechanistic
materialism of the French eighteenth century, and a
losing sight of the rich Marxist dialectic of the relationships of base and superstructure in history. Gilbert Mury
pertinently reminds us in this regard that 'the dialectic
of form and content is not reducible in Marxism to the
Aristotelian conception of the relations of form and
matter.' The relation of form to content, in the historical
problem which occupies us here, is a relation between
base and superstructure. Marx and Engels emphasized—

[19] *ibid.*, p. 65.
[20] *ibid.*, p. 66.

and it is this which distinguishes their materialism from all others—the dialectical character of this relation: base engenders superstructure, superstructure acquires a 'relative independence' in relation to base, and finally exerts an action in return upon base.

As a result, this imperfect criticism of religion, rooted in the traditions of eighteenth-century anti-clericalism and materialism, implies the abandonment of the essential element in Marxian materialism: the dialectic.

This 'reductionist' conception of Marxism, in which spiritual 'forms' 'are nothing but . . .' the base which has engendered them, would also lead to the denial of the subjective moment (as Lenin used to say) which constitutes Marxism itself, just as if the revolutionary attitude 'were nothing but . . .' the objective existence of the proletariat.

Exactly what, then, can this 'force' consist in, if the Christian 'faith', as protest and openness to the future, is distinguished, as Engels distinguishes it, into institution on the one hand and ideology on the other?

Engels points out, for example, that Christianity was incapable of conquering the other spiritual currents in the hellenistic world either by the force of the institution —before Constantine, Christianity was the religion of slaves and of the powerless and oppressed, or by the force of its ideology—from the end of the first century, Christianity, because of its syncretism, appeared to be an eclectic, confused and 'absurd' whole, when compared with the great intellectual systems of Greece and Rome.

This force, antecedent to institution and ideology, is faith. What I mean by faith, in this instance, is not a particular way of *representing* the world to oneself (for this is ideology), but a particular way of *standing up* before the world, of behaving in it, of living in it: the tension of a person totally committed to the 'drama', in Politzer's meaning of the term. Prior to any ideological contamination, the Christian faith consisted precisely in the living certainty that, because of the coming of Christ, his death on the cross, and his resurrection, the whole of life and the world itself could be changed, that man, redeemed from sin, had 'emerged' from the cosmos into which Greek humanism had plunged him, and that everything had become possible. The gap was open.

It is true that, in the conditions which prevailed at the time of its appearance, the faith which took hold of the powerless masses assumed the form of a messianic hope, an apocalyptic revenge by the humiliated and the injured against the powerful and the rich, against the decadent and oppressive Empire, the 'beast out of the abyss'.

But in different historical conditions, of which we have seen an example in the Peasant War of the sixteenth century, this behavioural structure, this faith, could be reactivated, and this 'protest' could become militant and revolutionary.

In today's historical conditions, it is no exaggeration to say that, if the existence of the Constantinian institution still weighs heavily and generally acts as a curb on the expansion of the struggle for advancement, faith is nonetheless at the very root of the determination of millions of Christians to struggle against exploitation and oppression.

Spontaneous protest against a world without justice is a constituent part of their faith.

But, as Gilbert Mury correctly emphasizes, this spontaneous protest of Christian faith, which underlies the progressive stands against war, colonialism, high-handedness, and social injustice, still puts it in no way on the same level as the revolutionary attitude. And for a crucial reason: the revolutionary attitude, properly speaking is not a spontaneous attitude. It stems from the boomerang of scientific socialism upon proletarian experience. Precisely because of its spontaneous character, the Christian protest, even when subjectively revolutionary, can easily alternate between reformism and anarchical revolt. It is this which explains the attraction exerted by Marxism on militant Christians who feel the need of its methods of thoughts, action and organization to achieve a real and effective insertion of their faith into history.

This realization of the Christian contribution to civilization and culture, and of the revolutionary potential of the faith, has been operative not only within the French Communist Party since the great step forward in 1937 but also within all Communist and Labour parties, particularly in those countries where progressive movements were taking shape within the Catholic Church and where, as a result, a fraternity of militant action was created between Marxists and Christians, as in Italy and Spain.

We can see an example of this in the speech which Palmiro Togliatti delivered at Bergamo in March, 1963, when he advanced four theses which constitute a distinguished contribution to the thinking of all Marxists on the problem of religion and relations with Christians.

1. 'With regard to the development of the religious conscience,' Togliatti declared, 'we do not accept the naïve and erroneous view that the advance of knowledge and the change in social structure are sufficient to bring about radical alterations. This view, which is the product of Enlightenment philosophy and eighteenth-century materialism, has not stood the test of time. The roots of religion go much deeper.'

2. 'It is not true that the religious conscience necessarily constitutes an obstacle to the appreciation and accomplishment of the duties and perspectives (of the building of socialism) and to adherence to this struggle. On the contrary, we think that the longing for a socialist society can not only find its way to men of religious faith, but can also find stimulus in the religious conscience itself when it is faced with the dramatic problems of today's world.'

3. 'By freeing believers and unbelievers of the yoke of the capitalist system, the realization of Communism (that is, a classless society) will give practical reality to the moral values which are shared by the Christian and Marxist conceptions of society and of man.'

4. 'Not only will the religious conscience be respected, but it will also have before it a real democratic field of growth, within which all historically positive values can find expression and make their contribution to the nation's progress.'

The Tenth Congress of the Italian Communist Party officially adopted the essential elements of these theses.

Within the Spanish Communist Party, research has a similar orientation. In November 1963, Santiago Carillo had declared: 'If, in our march towards the suppression of exploitation, with the hammer and sickle as our standard, there are others who accompany us with the cross, we bid them welcome.' Commenting on Carillo's remarks in *Realidad* for August 1965, Manuel Azcarate, another Spanish Communist leader, wrote: 'This implies that Christianity can be a standard, an ideal, which is capable of helping one group of Spaniards to fight against exploitation and for the victory of socialism. It implies, on the theoretical level, that we have seen the last of the narrow dogmatic views which presented the religious fact in one-sided fashion, seeing in it only that aspect which makes it a curb on and an obstacle to human progress.'

Azcarate stresses the practical consequences of this approach, particularly the guarantee that, in the future, neither persecution nor administrative repression will stem from such principles. If religion is everywhere and always considered as an opium of the people, the most effective means of doing away with it will inevitably have to be sought. But if the Marxists lay claim to the heritage of values introduced into human history by the activity and thought of men through religious meditation, and if they expect mutual enrichment from dialogue with Christians, persecution then becomes, in their own eyes, an alienating factor and would occasion impoverishment and mutilation for Marxism itself.

This is the safest foundation for dialogue and the best guarantee of its honesty: the deep-seated certainty that if each of us takes stock of what is basic in his convictions, he will discover, the one in his faith in God and the other in his faith in his task as a man, a mutual willingness to stretch man's creative energies to the maximum for the sake of realizing a total man, and he will become aware of the mutual enrichment which will flow from dialogue, co-operation and rivalry between the Marxists' Promethean humanism and Christian humanism.

If it is to be fruitful, this dialogue must be demanding.

The greatest danger is to idealize it, that is, to think that all other problems are solved and that the dialogue of a few 'noble souls'—disincarnate—will bring to the world the unity which is its salvation.

Let us be clearly aware of the fact that we are still only at the start of a great turning point in the epic of man.

The turning point itself will not be reached until we have graduated from the meetings of a few lonely pioneers, possibly even suspect in their own communities, to the authentic dialogue of the communities themselves.

The road is heavily ambushed and—once again, restricting myself to what a French Marxist can experience and report—we must confess that present political conditions do not make any the easier the requisite clarification of the problems.

On the level of institution (that is the Church's), it is undoubtedly true that Communists have learned to distinguish various strains within the positions—still socially and politically conservative, as a general rule—adopted: the excesses of the theological *intégrisme* which is usually linked, in politics, to the most reactionary movements; the reformist fancies of the Christian parties which are always drawn by anti-Communism to the impossible and harmful vision of third forces; and the authentic innovating currents of those Christians who have decisively opted for the future. But the political atmosphere, in France, for example, is tainted by the attempt, twice repeated in twenty-five years, to profit from each defeat of democracy by creating segregation among schools, as if the spread of the faith depended more on the state and its influence than on the prophetic power of the Christian message within a system of public schools, as open to Catholic teachers as to any others, and welcoming all children without reservation. This problem is surely one of the greatest obstacles to healthy development of the dialogue.

We find parallel difficulties on the ideological level. There is, for example, a constantly recurring effort to exploit—not, this time, democracy's sporadic backslidings

—the temporary lacunae and growth-crises in science, in order to base a fragile apologetic on them and thereby discredit, by contaminating it with the most outdated irrationality, the 'supernatural' in its most beautiful and authentic sense: that of the surpassing of nature. This obfuscation of faith by superstition is yet another obstacle to dialogue.

Finally, on the very level of faith, that is, the way in which the Gospel message is lived, there is at times a pathetic divorce and, to judge by its appearance to unbelievers, double expression of this faith: the one is turned away from the world so as to win purity for itself, while the other is immersed in the world, through research, work and conflict, so as to win the world for purity.

This dualism also disturbs and baffles us.

I know that, in regard to Communism, some Christians or other could just as easily point out all that conceals our own true face on the levels of institution, ideology and even faith. I have no difficulty in imagining most of the objections myself.

But, on both sides, the obstacles and the failures in understanding will only be removed by the passage from anathema to dialogue.

For our own part, we accept this dialogue and we desire it with all our strength.

We offer a dialogue without prejudice or hindrance.

We do not ask anyone to stop being what he is. What we ask is on the contrary, that he be it more and that he be it better. We hope that those who engage in dialogue with us will demand the same of us.

Dialogue with Christians implies, on their part, no religious concession whatever.

We have said it before and we say it again, because it

is so essential: as pressure increases among the Christian masses to reject any theological intrusion in the scientific realm, to stop seeing in technical and scientific progress a temptation of Satan but to see it as a legitimate assertion of man's power and greatness, to stop canonizing class hierarchy and social inequality as institutions willed by God in expiation of sin, to stop viewing private ownership of the means of production as a necessary guarantee of the freedom of the human person, to stop hurling anathemas at socialism and Communism but to see in them a form of organization of social relations which is superior to that of capitalism, to stop viewing the love of life, learning and happiness as some suspect sort of concupiscence; as this pressure from the Christian masses becomes sufficiently strong to loosen and to shatter the grip of the economic and political forces which link the Church's destiny with that of their own privileges, a vast panorama of battle and of work together opens out before us.

As far as faith is concerned, whether faith in God or faith in our task, and whatever our difference regarding its source—for some, assent to a call from God; for others, purely human creation—faith imposes on us the duty of seeing to it that every man becomes a man, a flaming hearth of initiative, a poet in the deepest sense of the word: one who has experienced, day by day, the creative surpassing of himself—what Christians call his transcendence and we call his authentic humanity.

This ideal is exalted enough and difficult enough of achievement to demand the combined efforts of all of us, even if we have to see the burning away—in the fire of dialogue which allows us to meet, deep within ourselves, on the threshold of the basic—of everything in us which prevents us from becoming what we are. This is the

glorious meaning which Nazim Hikmet has given to the
flame of purification and sacrifice:

> *If I do not burn,*
> *If you do not burn,*
> *If we do not burn,*
> *How shall the shadows*
> *Become light?*

Christian Promise and Revolution
by J. B. Metz

I can refer here only to some few points in Professor Garaudy's book. I should like to select those which touch directly upon fundamental theological questions. None of us will be able to make light of what is said there. Least of all, we theologians. Hence if my remarks have a pronounced critical character, they are not meant to deny blindly and dogmatically that this is an occasion, not merely to contradict and to complain, but also to listen attentively and to learn with a readiness for self-correction. I hope finally that my sketch of the theological position itself reveals something of that readiness of theology to listen critically to its Marxist partners in the discussion which leads neither to unimaginative adaptation nor to unreceptive rigidity, but to that fruitful conflict at which our dialogue aims and in which theology seeks to maintain its loyalty to the message with which it is charged precisely by sharing with the utmost determination the problems and queries of the world around it.

I shall try in this dialogue to approach in a critical spirit the essentials of our mutually opposed theories. I am very grateful to Professor Garaudy for saying that this essential and always unique reality cannot be the object of a hasty compromise. Our dialogue is not an 'exchange of feelings'; it promotes, not appeasement, but critical provocation. Only in this way perhaps can it lead the partners in the discussion at every turn to transform *themselves* and not to persist in out-of-date, liberalistic attitude, content with everything and seeking to agrees with everyone because it no longer possesses any productive imagination or power to change.

Professor Garaudy recognizes sincerely the decisive contribution which Christianity has made to the humanization of mankind. But he likewise reproaches it insistently for having contributed not a little to a dangerous mythicizing of human existence.

First of all, and wholly within the tradition of Marxist criticism of religion, he sees in Christianity an expression of the fact that man does not resist the infinite question which he is and the infinite need which drives him on, but provides for himself answers and fulfilments beyond history. He does this by hypostatizing his infinite questioning on the Deity, by objectivizing his wishes in a heaven in the hereafter, and so on. Now at least contemporary Christianity is itself aware of criticism of religion and of myth. It is aware of the fact that myths (in the negative sense understood here) may arise out of an inclination to find answers when for our part there is nothing to answer; that myths may obscure the duty of realizing historical existence and of finding historical answers. And frequently Christianity has been and is itself in danger of incurring the suspicion of mythology, because of an apparent superfluity of answers and a failure to ask genuinely painful questions. But was not this danger always recognized in Christianity, which always comprised some sort of 'negative theology'? Let us examine a little more closely however the objection that biblical religion in its conception of God hypostatizes the unfulfilled expectations of man.

How is God attested in the Bible? Here I can cite only one series of biblical statements, directly linked with our question. In my opinion, it is very clearly expressed in the Old Testament account of the revelation of God in Exodus 3.14. Certainly God is there said to be our future, but *our* future in so far as this future belongs to *itself*, is grounded in itself, and is not simply the correlative of our wishes and strivings: 'I will be who I will be', runs the central phrase of the passage mentioned. It defines the deity of God as free, self-belonging dynamism of our future and not primarily as 'Being above us', in the sense of a beyond that is to be experienced outside history.

Thus understood, God appears not as the product of impatience with our own wishes or as a result of resignation to the impossibility of fulfilling our infinite strivings; he appears not as a damping of man's historical initiative, but precisely as liberation for this initiative. For only a future which is *more* than the projection of our own open or latent possibilities can really call us out beyond ourselves (Professor Garaudy also demands this of man and describes it as his destiny); only this can free us for the really 'new' which does not hurl us back again into what Ernst Bloch called the 'melancholy of fulfilment'; it can free us for what has never yet been.

Such a conception of God takes away the force of the suspicion that God is only an alienated idea and an idea constantly alienating us, of our own historical existence. Indeed, this alone makes possible historical existing. It makes the world appear as a world of history rising towards this 'new' reality, in the process of which our freedom is involved. Being orientated towards this new reality, this biblical faith in promise arouses a revolutionary attitude to the world—as long as revolution is characterized by a lively awareness of an absolute *Novum*, which cannot be understood simply as the evolutive projection of our own possibilities.

Once we recall this aspect (which admittedly has not been greatly emphasized) of the biblical faith in promise, can there really then be any talk of this faith making man relax in his historical struggle, of its having a purely comforting and tranquillizing tendency? Is not our modern conception of the world, with its persistent will for the 'new', with its primacy of the future, rooted precisely in this biblical faith? Professor Garaudy has frequently defined Marxism as a 'theory of historical initiatives': is not this definition based on a conception of the world such as that which becomes apparent precisely in the biblical faith in promise? When I say this, I do not mean to deceive, nor do I wish to adopt Marxism by following some devious route. The concrete historical connections and differences have quite other dimensions and the question of truth in our controversy cannot be decided by the evidence of historical causalities.

Nevertheless I should like to supplement and continue my previous reflections with a critical observation. Can we really criticize every faith in promise as a disastrous alienation and concealment of the radical nature of man's questioning state, as a dangerous myth which attempts to formulate and to fix as answers what exists for us solely as questions? Is there not a faith in promise which does not blunt the questioning state, but sharpens it? How for instance can man's questioning turn into an historical demand, unless it is guided by a promise? How and by what means can this questioning become historical initiative if it does not possess an under-current of hope, the 'warm current of hope', as Bloch would say? How is it that the question does not remain in the order of pure contemplation of the world, of the extension of speculative knowledge? how is it that it does not remain purely philosophical? What impels it to become revolutionary, world-changing, to seize historical initiatives, to understand the world altogether as an emergent world of history oriented to the future? Does not a primacy of hope make itself felt here in the questioning state of humanity itself? But hope contains a superfluity of trust and historical imagination, of which it does not allow itself to be deprived by any total criticism of religion and myth.

In my opinion there exists even among theologians a desire totally to de-mythologize the Christian message of promise, to reduce its content of hope to an empty, symbolic paraphrase of human questionability as such. But it is precisely in this way that this hope is deprived of any genuine character of conflict and contradiction in regard to the particular reality existing at the time, and thus robbed of its power to move history. For history is kept going—if at all—not through the obvious fact of the universal questionability of human existence, but through what is not obvious, through the 'impossible', through the object of our hope.

In connection with the foregoing, I should like to say a word about the Christian doctrine of the Last Days, in order to show that the alternative worked out by Professor Garaudy between promise and demand, between expectation and conflict, and even, within limits, between Christian eschatological hope and revolutionary world-formation, does not exist or at any rate ought not to exist for the Christian. For Christian hope can never be realized in purely contemplative expectation. Nor— and, indeed, least of all—as hope stemming from the cross. For pure contemplation of its nature refers always to what has been and is at all times existent. But the future of the world, rooted in the cross of Christ, which is the aim and object of Christian hope, is also a reality still emerging and still to come. Therefore this hope must be essentially creative and militant; it must therefore be realized in a creative, in a sense productive, eschatology. It is always hope as awaiting *and* as struggle. For faith according to the New Testament is always a victory, a victory not only over ourselves, but—according to John— a victory overcoming the world. The imperative of this faith—'not to conform ourselves to this world'—'means', Moltmann has observed, 'not only to transform ourselves, but to change in resistance and creative expectation the shape of the world in which we believe, hope and love.'

The primitive community of the New Testament was wholly pervaded by its expectation of the closeness of the Last Days *and* by its universal missionary mandate: it is a community of expectation *and* mission—indeed, of expectation *in* the mission. Eschatological expectation as reflected in the attitude of this primitive community is a militant, world-changing expectation. Expectation of the approaching kingdom had nothing paralyzing about it; it was seen as liberating and challenging in relation to the world.

In the consciousness of this community Jesus was not the teacher of a *Weltanschauung*; he was not a guide, a world-expounder and world-interpreter, but a revolutionary who—acting, suffering—was in conflict with the existing social order of the world and in the service of his world-transforming mission for that reason did not need admirers, but imitators. The kingdom proclaimed by him does not simply lie ready before us as a distant goal, existing already in all essentials, merely concealed as yet, to which we are linked in the pure conception of our longing. This eschatological city of God is rather itself still in the process of emerging. By approaching it in hope we work at its construction: we are builders— not merely interpreters—of a future, of which God himself is the dynamism.

The Vatican Council's new constitution *On the Church* says: 'The world is irrevocably set on the renewal which is anticipated in a real way in this life'. The Christian must therefore consider himself a 'fellow-worker' in this 'new world' of universal peace and justice. The orthodoxy of his faith must constantly 'justify' itself in the orthopraxy of his action on the world, directed to the last end: for the truth promised is a truth that must be 'done', as John (cf. 3.21) very clearly inculcates. The Christian himself must create in the world conditions in which this promised truth counts, is with him, is present: he must take part himself in changing his world. The Christian eschatology, therefore, is not a pure eschatology for the present time in which all passion for the future is turned into making present of eternity—as out of this world—in the individual moment of existence. But neither is it an eschatology of purely passive expectation for which the world and its time appear as a kind of waiting room, prepared in advance, in which we should have to sit around, uncommitted and bored—the more hopefully, so much the more bored—until the door of God's audience chamber opens. Christian eschatology must be understood rather as a productive and militant eschatology. Christian hope is a hope at which—as Ernst Bloch once very neatly observed, we 'have not only something to drink, but also something to cook'. Eschatological faith and earthly commitment do not exclude, but imply one another.

I know that this sounds like a lot of talk about 'principles'. Has the Church then really fought for her promises? Or—more precisely—has she always made clear in a credible way for *what* promises she fights? Has she in fact brought it home credibly that the promises she proclaims, the hope to which she witnesses, is not a hope in the Church, but in the kingdom of God as the future of the world, in a kingdom of universal peace and justice (cf. 2 Peter 3.13), where there are no more tears and in which there will be no 'mourning nor crying nor pain any more' (Rev. 21.4)? And has she in creative-militant expectation gone all out for *this* promise? For the promise of the Sermon on the Mount, which makes her always the Church of the poor and oppressed? Here we must face a questioning which reaches right down to the roots of our Christian existence. And in this respect we shall not get any further without a painful conversion.

Of course the promises which shine out in Christ are indeed a stimulus in all our militant striving towards the future, but they are a spur that does not simply drive these movements on to the future in a mood of militant secular optimism, but also opposes them critically in the name of afflicted and affronted man. Because of the scandal of the cross, Christian faith in promise can never become simply an ideological paraphrase of the modern militant sense of progress; it can never simply canonize the technical-economic-social progress brought about— rightly—by ourselves. It is and always remains the expression of a militant hope—against all hope. And in this respect it is and remains essentially 'untimely': untimely, however, not in the sense of those who remain forever in the past, of the grumblers and those burdened with resentment, but untimely in a productive sense. In relation to our movements towards the future its function and its dynamism is both critical and liberating.

Karl Rahner has formulated it in this way: 'The Church must not try to fulfil this 'critical' function merely by delivering this criticism as it were from outside to man in his movement towards a future of his own creation; rather must it show him how this criticism emerges out of his own experience of the way into his own intra-mundane future. It must tell him that the growth of what has been planned always involves also an increase in the unplanned and unforeseen; that the sacrifice for the future of the generations to come loses its meaning and dignity and therefore also its force in the long run, if this sacrifice considers men living at the moment merely as material and the means for building up the future, without regard to the absolute value, the right and dignity of men living at the present time. . . . The Church has to warn against those utopias which are not the beginning of a real future, but the programme of the shaping of a future which is unrealistic and there-fore—when the attempt is made to realize it—compels us slowly (for the sake of "face-saving" on the part of such a false ideology), with great sacrifices and losses to correct again what has been planned wrongly.'

Christianity must understand its faith in promise as just such a critical and liberating force, which also con-stantly takes the ritual out of a forced sense of progress. Of course this faith in promise must not then become—as so often—an ideology of the future. The poverty of its knowledge of this future must be dear to it. What distinguishes it from the conceptions of the future of Eastern and Western origin is that of itself it knows not more, but *less* about the future of mankind we are seek-ing, and that it keeps to the poverty of this knowledge. 'By faith Abraham obeyed when he was called to go out to a place which he was to receive as an inheritance; and he went out, not knowing where to go' (Heb. 11.8). This faith in promise must always also include a 'negative theology' of the future.

From this standpoint I would like to criticize the idea of 'total man', with which Professor Garaudy defined the Marxist conception of the future, as a problematic abstraction and simultaneously as excessive questioning about the future. Does not every vision of a future autonomous, perfected humanity break down in man himself? Does not his more sober understanding take its revenge again and again on such visions and plans imposed on him? Do we not clearly perceive that the technical hominization of the world which we have organized, the process of turning its possibilities into availabilities, is still far from producing unambiguously its increasing humanization (and does not the dangerous illusion of Marxism lie precisely in the attempt to make these two processes parallel)? Do we not know too well that, even as men of a finally hominized world, we shall always go on asking for the human reality still to come? It is the question already raised in Isaiah:

> 'Watchman, what of the night?'
> The watchman says:
> 'Morning comes, and also the night.
> If you will inquire, inquire;
> come back again.'   (Isa. 21.11-12).

In Professor Garaudy's thought the question constantly recurs as to whether Christianity is not in fact a form of man's dangerous self-alienation. Who would deny—I would not—that in the name of Christianity and the Church such a self-alienation of man has not rarely at least been protected? The fact, for instance, that particular social groupings were canonized in the name of Christianity and that for the poor and oppressed comforting words about the hereafter were all too speedily and abundantly available? The fact that the Church made her criticism of the mighty in this world often far too softly and frequently much too late?

It must not be said that this is a question of tactics or opportunity. It is a question of historical responsibility, if there is even a grain of truth in the statement of Camus: that there were times in which every sin was a mortal sin, every indifference a crime. The Church asserts very clearly and decisively the claim to be the guardian of 'natural law'. But has she always equally clearly and decisively fulfilled the obligation arising out of this: to defend with all lawful means the humanity of *all* men? Is not the question of so-called 'natural law' —prior to all purely theoretical problems—a crisis of confidence in Christianity's universal humanitarian commitment, 'without respect of persons'? Here history accuses and we have to take this accusation seriously, particularly since Christianity as historical reality always has to defend its own concrete historical developments.

The question however remains as to whether Christianity of its nature fosters such an evil self-alienation of man or whether it really tries to fix only those 'self-alienations' which cannot be dissolved by any amount of social progress. Let us for once leave aside the question as to whether the word 'self-alienation'—which cannot be dissociated from an individualistic romantic humanism—is a suitable designation of the state of affairs which is important for our question. Are there really only self-alienations which—as Marxism supposes—can be overcome by social efforts and which we Christians canonize with the aid of theology of the hereafter and of original sin? Are there not rather forms of human self-alienation which cannot be dissolved by lifting them out of the economic-social situation—no matter how successfully—and from which man will always draw the 'pain of his finiteness'? Are there not self-alienations which cannot simply be reduced to the effect of a social, utopian expectation?

Let us assume for once that the great social utopias in East and West were realized and had led to a far-reaching freedom of man from economic determination in the future great society. Would then man's questioning confrontation with himself be at an end? Or would it not for the first time force itself on us in a radical fashion, since then—*ex supposito*—many things lapse which also divert us from this confrontation and soften it: such things, for instance, as work and economic interest? What are we to do, for example, about the problem of guilt or of evil? Or what is the meaning of the experience to which we theologians give the odd name, 'concupiscence'? In this theological catchword there is expressed the experience of a self-alienation which evidently is not open to a purely economic solution of the problem.

We experience within us a constant discrepancy between that to project ourselves towards and that for which we actually live, between the idea of our life and how we live it. We experience, for example, what might have been for us an occasion of transformation—a great sorrow, perhaps. In the long run it is levelled down by us to our everyday experience with its readiness for compromise; we discover that pain also does not transform us, that for this too we seek and find a bourgeois solution and degrade everything to the obviousness of our dull ordinary lives. Camus once expressed what I mean in this way: 'It seems as if great souls are sometimes less dismayed by pain itself than by the fact that it does not last'. In such and similar experiences we become aware of a form of self-alienation which cannot be overcome simply by economic means. And, to mention once again the unique example, what is to be made of the experience of suffering and death?

If we take Professor Garaudy at his word in regard to what he has said or quoted about death, then—with all due respect for the idealism of his conception—for me there arises the question: is not this conception of death exposed at least to the same extent to the suspicion of mythicizing and mystifying mortal existence, with which he reproaches the Christian conception? What is this dying into the totality of future mankind?

The Christian sees in death an experience of the threat to his existence, of radical self-alienation, which he hopes to endure only in solidarity with Jesus, the crucified and risen, and which he understands only within that horizon which is opened to him for this purpose by the message of Jesus. In this certainly, it seems to me, is also included that element of the understanding of death which Professor Garaudy's theory rightly tries to bring home to us: namely, the essential removal from this death-situation of its private character, the essential reference of this experience of death to other human beings. Similarly, the Christian attitude to death must not be narrowed down to an individualistic aloofness from the world. It also looks towards the world, the world of our brethren. It implies a self-forgetting outpouring of love for others, for the 'least of these', implies selfless defence of *their* hope. For the endurance of death in anticipation takes place within this hopeful love. 'We know that we have passed from death into life, because we love the brethren' (1 John 3.14). Christian hope draws victoriously to itself the passion of death, which menaces our promises, accepting the venture of brotherly love towards the least—in imitation of Christ, whose being was once very impressively defined by Bonhoeffer as 'being there for others'.

The value of a humanism is ultimately decided—in my opinion—by the hermeneutic and productive power it develops for those frontier situations in human existence, those 'self-alienations' for which there can be no simple and purely social solutions: for guilt, concupiscence, death. Do we really find in Marx a more instructive answer to these questions than we do in Jesus? A predominant note in Professor Garaudy's arguments on this theme nevertheless seems to me to be of particular importance and even more especially indispensable for a Christian anthropology. This is the development of the awareness that I, as an individual, can realize my hope only by trying to make over such a hope to others; the development of the awareness that I can realize my freedom only as concrete decision for others' freedom—against every form of enslavement of man.

Professor Garaudy has very clearly insisted that the Marxist alternative to religion is not the materialistic atheism which Christian scholasticism tries to refute, but a humanism determined totally and with absolute steadfastness on the 'redemption of man's honour'. According to him, therefore, the Marxist attitude does not really imply direct unbelief, which takes the form only of the explicit negation of faith and its manifestation in religion. Marxism therefore presents itself not primarily as a project of the world and of existence directed *against God*, but as the offer of a possibility of positive existence, of a total humanity *without God*. Thematic atheism is therefore not really the object, but the presupposition of Marxism. I do not at all want to suggest that this *un-*

belief of an age that is to a certain extent post-atheistic is less shattering than explicitly atheist unbelief. Nevertheless, in my opinion, it is just here that we are offered a chance of responsible discussion and exchange of views.

Christianity must take this humanitarian claim literally and make its solidarity in the struggle for man's humanity more decisively known than ever before. Threatened man: this might be the point at which the truth—as between belief and unbelief—today is tested, at which it is brought to light. Here the Church—which expressly described itself at the Second Vatican Council as the 'Church of the poor and afflicted'—and with her all Christianity has to do justice to a great claim. Nothing could be more deceptive than for the Church to try to give the impression that nothing more was at stake for it here and that it had nothing more to lose in this dialogue on the 'redemption of man's honour'. There can be no premature purely religious or theological modification of the historical responsibility imposed on her by her faith in promise: this in the end would only betray the fact that Christianity itself in the struggle for man no longer ventures anything new or creative and therefore abruptly takes the sting out of this fight.

In the struggle for man, in the form it takes today, Christianity can no longer (in the name of the 'unworldliness of faith') be concerned exclusively with the private subjectivity of the individual or the private intimacy of the interpersonal I-thou experience. Does not Christianity in fact through its exclusive concentration on subjectivity and the inter-personal sphere enter into a dangerous privacy and arbitrariness in regard to the unceasing evolution of the world? Is faith, by its tendency to be purely subjective and existential, not in danger of losing precisely the provocative force of its responsibility for the world which fidelity to the message of Jesus constantly demands of it?

The cross of Jesus, from which faith receives its orientations and promises, is in the last resort not something belonging to the intimate depths of the purely individual-personal sphere. Nor does it belong to the most sacred part of the purely religious; it belongs beyond the threshold of the sheltered private or screened religious sphere: it is 'outside', as the Epistle to the Hebrews says, in the profane world, as a scandal to this, as folly and as promise. Therefore faith must take part in the struggle for one world; it must be involved in the public, the social, the concrete history of this world. It must not continue to make what is socially provocative in the message of Jesus purely individualistic and private ('modern' as the tendency may be in theology at the present time, radical demythologizing would make faith and salvation a wholly private affair.

Because of its relationship to the main contents of the biblical promise, the task is of linking itself with the world as society and with the world-changing, revolutionary forces in that society constantly imposed on Christian faith. It must come to terms with the great political-social Utopias, with the promises of a universal peace and economic justice ripening in our modern society.

This has nothing to do with some dubious introduction of political activity into Christianity and the Church. On the contrary! It is only by being aware of their public responsibility that faith and Church can undertake their critical function in society. Only in this way does the Church avoid becoming a mere ideological superstructure over a particular, existing order of society. Only in this way does she avoid becoming a pleasant travesty of pure power-politics. Only in this way of course does she also avoid becoming the 'last religion' of our completely secularized society: a religion entrusted indeed with certain therapeutic function for the individual, but no longer with any power to criticize society.